OLD FORGE

FALL OUT
ROMAN CATHOLICS
AND JEWS

by
ANTHONY HAIG-THOMAS
Fg.Off. RAF (Retd)

A personal account of this distinguished officer's
Royal Air Force Career 1956-1963
with a bit added on

First Edition 2008

Designed
by
Jupper Peep
www.jupperpeep.com

Published
by
Old Forge Publishing
39 Backgate
Cowbit
Lincolnshire
PE12 6AP
oldforgepub@aol.com
www.oldforgepublishing.org
01406 381313

ISBN 978-1-906183-04-2

Printed for Old Forge Publishing
By
LPPS Ltd
Wellingborough
Northants
NN8 3PJ

01933 270411

Contents

FALL OUT
ROMAN CATHOLICS
AND JEWS

PREFACE

My father wrote, and had published, his autobiography at the age of 26 so, while I was ADC to the AOC 11 Group, aged 23, I thought I would upstage him, write my own, and started to do so. Nearly fifty years later I found my early pathetic attempt and decided to rewrite and finish it; in doing so I have tried to convey my very young and immature attitude to life. It was a life filled with those twin highlights of my late teens and early twenties, flying and sex, in that order – just – and I have tried to write those years as I felt them at the time with an appropriate degree of immaturity. Few people read meticulously kept diaries and, when published, they have to be transcribed and précised to a narrative form. I kept no diary but the contemporary notes from my failed first autobiographical attempt have helped jog the memory. As a pilot, I have my own logbooks, now bound in a tasteful dark green leather, with which to relive my youth on rainy days.

With enormous thanks to Martin Barraclough, Karen Wilsher, Tony Podmore and an unknown author. Martin for proof reading the original illiterate script, Karen for typing and retyping and retyping and Tony for numerous attempts to satisfy my mapping requirements. Together they spent far more time on my magnum opus than I did. I must mention the unknown author because decades ago I read a book, written in the present tense and the first person singular, of a night fight in a 'fifties' jet. I forget the author and the title of the book but I have copied his style in the first chapter unashamedly, but alas without his literacy skills; it was beautifully written.

A. Haig-Thomas
January 2007

FOREWORD

Tony joined the Royal Air Force five years before I did, and so the Air Force that he encountered as a very young man was very similar to the one that I knew at the same age. It was an Air Force where flying was still plentiful and where, not many years on from WW 2, deaths in flying accidents were accepted as regrettable, but routine and to be expected. It was an Air Force that was populated by a rich, but gradually fading, tapestry of characters who would not have fitted into today's more business-orientated and very serious organisation.

Tony brings all this to life with vivid prose, not only telling his highly personal story of a young man in hog-heaven (well, most of the time) but also painting an affectionate and authentic picture of that Air Force that, like him, I knew and loved so well. Some of his descriptions of flying are lyrical. Passages on operational flying in Venoms and Hunters out of Aden (and ground operations with the Army) are exciting and, I suspect, play down the gallantry involved.

If you know what it was like to be in the Royal Air Force in the late 50s and early 60s, then you must wallow in the nostalgia generated by Tony's story. If you would like to know what the Air Force was like in those days, then read this book, because it is the real thing. If you are just curious to know more about Tony, then much will be revealed by this book. I thought that I knew him pretty well – now I think I understand him!

John Allison

Air Chief Marshal Sir John Allison KCB, CBE, RAF (Retd)

Chapter I

A VENOM TO HEAVEN

It is an overcast night, the date is July 15th 1959 and I am 21; there is an all pervasive and suffocating heat that only those who have lived in Aden can imagine.I drag down the harness in my Venom FB4 until it bites into my shoulders, my hands run round the familiar pre-start cockpit drills and then, moments later, the stillness is shattered by the cartridge starter, and the dark by an orange glow behind me, as the Ghost engine lights up, a little wet, and, for a few seconds, the flickering light of hot jet fuel illuminates the ground crew standing by the aircraft. The distinctive wailing sound of the engine, so common in the forties and fifties on airfields throughout the world, rises in pitch as I move slowly out of the 8 Squadron dispersal, down the long taxiway, to Khormaksar's main runway. Minutes later, safely airborne and off the noisy airfield frequency, the Venom punches a satisfying hole in the night sky at 360 knots; the soft glow from the instruments, under ultra-violet stimulation, absorbs my total attention as I close at 10,000 feet a minute on the 8/8 cloud cover.

It is just a sheet of stratus at 2000' and I do not expect it to be thick, even so I am quite unprepared to be through it in a few seconds to erupt on a world, so breathtaking, that the memory of it will remain with me all my life. A huge tropical full moon has risen and it is poised just a few inches above a sea of cloud that stretches to the horizon; my eyes, having accommodated to the darkness below, are particularly well adapted to absorb the scene completely. Easing back on the throttle I roll gently round the huge white orb and go low flying over the moonlit ocean until, in all too short a time, the fuel gauge shows 1,400lbs remaining from the 2,750 that I have taken off with as, for this sortie, my tip tanks have not been filled. I still have my briefed exercise to fly and, sadly, this does not include low flying over my private, moonlit, sea. I am to climb to 20,000 feet, home to overhead my base at Khormaksar just north of Aden, and then, after a controlled let down, to feed into a radar approach. A low level overshoot is then to be flown from the runway threshold, with this followed by a turn down wind and a full-stop landing to complete the sortie.

Centrifugal engines, like the Ghost in my Venom, need very careful handling as there is no automatic acceleration control unit fitted and I need energy, which is speed, so I open the engine up slowly and smoothly to full power. The Venom now races low level across the sea towards the moon and, very soon, I have .65 indicated on my mach meter so I pull smoothly back on the stick until 4G is registered on the accelerometer. The aircraft passes the vertical, the G loading falls off, and I am then facing back, down-moon, into a dark night sky. A short pause in the inverted, a deft left deflection of the stick with my right wrist, to roll upright and I am now heading in the general direction of my base. I can relax now, settle down to some instrument flying, and just do as the controller tells me, until the lights at the end of the runway appear, at which time more demanding handling skills will again be required of me.

Now, on the ground at Khormaksar, every time I transmit, a little line will jump out from the centre of the controller's cathode-ray tube and, where it touches the circumference of his circular display, will be a number. This is the heading, in degrees, that I have to steer to guide me to the 'Khormaksar overhead'. I follow my instructions and, within three or four minutes, the controller again asks me to transmit. I do so and the little line on his tube wavers around the central spot indicating that I am overhead my base. The controller gives me an 'outbound' heading to steer and, a minute later, tells me to commence my descent. In the dark, still, silence of my cockpit I reduce my RPM to 6,000 and extend the airbrakes; a gentle vibration of the airframe tells me that they are deployed. The airspeed bleeds to 270 knots at which point I lower the nose and hold this speed until, at 12,000 feet, I start a left turn to align me with Khormaksar's runway 09. Now I am heading back up-moon and sinking fast to the layer of cloud; the Goddess herself is a little higher on the horizon but the wondrous sight is still there. I take a few seconds off my instruments to drink it in once more and then, like Count Dracula returning to the grave after a brief night of joy, I descend into the cloud.

Down on the ground the approach controller presses a 'talk' switch on an intercom to the radar operator. "I have a Venom at five miles, level at 2,000, steering 090°." The Approach controller waits until he has confirmation that the approach radar has me in good contact and then tells me to change my radio to the radar frequency. Operators of what was, in those days, called a GCA radar always had a wonderful, reassuring, level tone to their instructions. Tonight the quiet reassuring voice tells me to reduce speed and carry out my checks for landing. Back in the cockpit I emerge from the base of the cloud and, in the few seconds I allow myself off my instruments, can see the lights of Aden town dimly through the heat haze. I lower half flap, and then the undercarriage, feeling, as always, relief when I see the three little green lights appear to show that the wheels are down, and locked. When the speed gets to 120 knots I hold it there, with a little more power, at 8,000 RPM. The GCA Controller starts his patter. "Venom you are at five miles on centre line and approaching the glide path – do not acknowledge any further instructions." I again do as I am told and, at two miles, in the haze, I can just see the runway lights. "Venom, final check, confirm three greens." "Three greens," I reply. "Roger. Continue your descent, on centre line, and on glide path." Tonight, in the heat, the wind has fallen to a calm and this makes it easy, both for myself, and the controller. At one mile and around 300 feet, with the runway lights now clearly visible, I dispense with the controller's instructions and continue visually. He keeps up his steady monologue although his voice has now become just background noise. I select full flap and cross the runway threshold 5 knots fast, at 110, holding the aircraft steady with my right hand, while my left smoothly applies power. The engine produces 5,200 lbs of thrust at full power and my aircraft, with its fuel state now down to 800 lbs, only weighs around 9,000 so the acceleration, for an aircraft of its time, is very good; I raise my flaps to half-way and then the undercarriage. Although I am now back on instruments, through my peripheral vision, I feel, rather than see, the runway lights flashing past, and then blurring, to become a continuous stream of light. Suddenly I have left the airfield. Ahead, if I look out, is an inky blackness for I am now over the sea and, as looking out at 300 feet and 190 knots in an inky blackness, with nothing in front of me except the sea, is a sure way of dying, I again fly my aircraft on instruments. The radar controller hands me over to the tower as I turn through 180°, and now at 1,000 feet on the runway's reciprocal heading, I call "Venom down wind". It is a point of principle in the single-seat world to keep all RT transmissions as brief and clipped as possible so I avoid any unnecessary words. I complete my circuit visually, land, and taxi in, plunging back into the sauna heat of an Aden night as I open the hood and look for the marshaller's wands to guide me to my parking place. As I shut the High Pressure cock the wailing banshee behind me dies. My hands run through the familiar shut down procedure and the ground crew appear and replace the pin in my ejection seat. "Aircraft all right sir?" "Yes," I reply, wondering if it was possible for life to get any better.

Chapter 2

A BEGINNING

As I walked back to the mess to join the evening Bridge school, which was awaiting my return, I felt that all my training and efforts to get into the Royal Air Force had finally paid off. From the time of my earliest memories I had only ever wanted to fly aeroplanes. This was not surprising as my childhood was spent on the East Anglian Coast in wartime and the skies were full of fighters, barrage balloons, aircraft towing banners and great waves of bombers, the noise of which hung in the evening skies for half an hour as the formations joined up and headed for the Third Reich. At Ludgrove, my preparatory school, I had naturally been an avid and conspicuously unsuccessful aero modeller and then, while at Eton, I suffered a major setback. The Air Force operated a flying scholarship scheme, the interview and medical for which I regarded as a formality, so I was dumbfounded when I discovered that I had been 'rejected' not failed but 'rejected'! Apparently I had become short sighted and was unable to achieve the minimum standard with either eye.

No one will ever know the internal agonies I suffered as the end of my school days approached and my third rejection had come through from the Royal Air Force aircrew selection centre coupled with a firm note stating that I may not again apply for aircrew. In desperation I embarked on a course that looks pathetically naïve now; I wrote letters to any and every Senior Air Force Officer whose name I saw in a newspaper asking for help in overturning the Selection Centre's decision The result was predictable – they all replied kindly, and courteously, and said "Bad luck". Worse was to come. I was summoned to the recruiting centre at Reading; apparently I had written to two officers of very senior rank who had discovered the simultaneous approach; the recruiting Officer told me to cease writing to Air Force Officers. He then, in my presence, rang the ophthalmic department at Hornchurch who confirmed, as I listened, that Cadet Haig-Thomas could never be considered for aircrew, which seemed final enough. My next approach struck gold; while waiting for my train at Reading Station to return to Eton from the interview, I bought a copy of the Times and there, at the bottom of a page, was the announcement that an Air Commodore Neeley had been promoted to Air Vice Marshal and appointed Chief Consulting Ophthalmic Surgeon to the Royal Air Force.

As soon as I arrived back at school I dashed off another letter, in direct contravention to my instructions from Reading, and received a reply instructing me to call and see him at the Central Medical Establishment during the school holidays, at which appointment, and after further tests, he declared that I was substantially outside the minimum standards but, as I was exceptionally keen, he would authorise a special exception to be made. I was in and I was just eighteen.

First port of call in an RAF career for a pilot in the mid-fifties, following a few days signing on and the fitting of an RAF uniform at Cardington, was Kirton-in-Lindsey near Scunthorpe. Here, for three months, the air force moulded its raw material and eliminated around five percent of the students who had survived the weeding process at the aircrew selection centre. Here I did all the things expected of me; I got drunk for the first (and very nearly last) time, lost my virginity and, much more worrying, my rifle. While on the course all students were issued with a rifle, which had to be chained to the bed when it's owner was not on parade. The penalty for the loss of one's weapon is, as is well known, a full-blown military court martial. With this knowledge my terror can be imagined when ordered to fall in early one morning for a parade, with arms, to find that my rifle was not chained to my bed and was nowhere to be found. Corporal Davis, our NCO, was in his usual form, the only man before or since who has really terrified me. He ordered us to form up outside the barrack block with the rest of my course, they all with their rifles 'at ease', I with my hands behind my back. "Squad Attenshun, Slope Arms, Preezent Arms." Crash, Crash, Crash, went the drill movements; I was left standing to attention with all my colleagues presenting arms. I felt even more conspicuous as I was in the front row and now Corporal Davis came slowly down the line until he got to me, stopped, and ordered me to the guardroom with an escort. Was this the ignominious end of my air force career after only six weeks? The full might of military discipline swung into action until eventually Corporal Davis put me out of my agony and had me released from the guardroom. He said that he had found my rifle leaning in the corner of the lavatories in my barrack block where I had left it the previous evening and that he had taken it into custody. I never lost another rifle, but it cost me a weekends freedom to learn the lesson.

The course at Kirton-in-Lindsey lasted for three months and must have been a real shock for anyone who had not endured the hardships of a boarding school; I rather enjoyed it as it was the beginning of the fulfilment of my dream and the Air Force could do no wrong. The ninety-day service induction is, I suspect, standard to all the services and it works miracles, converting everything from Dukes to dustmen - there were both - into a homogenised product, ready to be trained in their specific individual roles.

The courses in those days were large as they had navigators, engineers and observers as well as pilots on them; the barrack block was polished and polished, boots were shined and uniforms pressed long into the night. On occasion one of the senior courses would come in late in the evening, when the work was nearly done, and 'trash' the whole place so that work had to start all over again. There were lectures on lots of subjects from mathematics to how to avoid unmentionable diseases; lots of drill, where I first discovered that I had (and still do have) rounded shoulders. The escape and evasion exercises were great fun but I still remember the cold when we had to camp out in the hills near Buxton in Derbyshire. I have never been so cold in my life before or since. It was also an exercise in demonstrated leadership. Everyone was frozen and had been sleep deprived because of the cold but at 0600 hrs precisely our CO, a Squadron Leader whose name shamefully I cannot recall, came down the line of tents bare foot, and in his pyjamas, to get us up. I couldn't believe anyone could survive like that. It was a great demonstration of leading by personal example and a very small act but it is perfectly remembered fifty years later.

At the end of the course some failed their examinations and left while, for the successful, the thrill of postings to the flying training schools were announced. Our Course was divided in half, one division going to Canada to fly first Harvards and then T33 Jets, the other half, which included me, being scheduled to fly Jet Provosts at Hullavington, near Chippenham in Wiltshire followed by an advanced course on Vampires for those that made the grade. Before we left however we had to 'draw' our flying kit and the dear old RAF fitted us out with all the kit needed to fly a Lancaster in World War II. Silk inner gloves with leather outers, leather helmets with goggles, sheepskin flying boots etc etc. Anyone who has seen the film of 'The Dambusters' will know what I mean. When we arrived at Hullavington it all had to be exchanged for contemporary flying suits, helmets and gloves. Most left Kirton-in-Lindsey with little regret. It was June 1956; I was homogenised, and together with nearly half of my course had lost my virginity to a couple of very obliging, strictly amateur, village lasses who understood cadet pilots' problems. Best of all I was an Acting Pilot Officer with my foot on the first rung of the ladder leading to Marshal of the Royal Air Force.

Chapter 3

WHITE MOUSE

In the early 1950s, when most front line aircraft were jet powered, it seemed anomalous to train pilots in the totally different field of big piston technology with superchargers, constant speed units, automatic boost control, cowling gills to cool the cylinder heads, radiator shutters, oil coolers, inter coolers, fuel in gallons and endurance in hours when they would be operational with Jet Pipe Temperatures, percentage RPM, and endurance in minutes. We were to fly the Jet Provost T.1, a jet version of the Piston Provost, to see if pilots could learn to fly jet aircraft from the beginning: the trials were coded 'White Mouse'. There were three courses and ours was the second. Hunting Aircraft built nine T.1 aircraft, eight of which we flew, with one retained for company development work; this latter aircraft still exists, and at the time of writing, 2006, is at North Weald. Being a jet the aircraft was of course much easier to fly than the piston engined Provost but, whereas the piston pilots needed handling skills, the Jetties had to cope with oxygen, retractable undercarriage, airbrakes and very little fuel. We had to climb through cloud, make cross country flights, and descend through cloud, solo, returning with no fuel for a diversion. Retrospectively I am amazed - and still cannot believe - how easily it was accomplished by all the students on No.120 (Jet) Course. I liked the 'Jet' bit – everyone else at Hullavington flew piston Provosts so we all, quite properly in our view, felt very superior. But the very best bit of being the crème de la crème was that we each had a free daily Penguin chocolate biscuit under the grand title of 'high energy rations for fighter aircrew'. When you are eighteen nothing gives more pleasure than getting right up the noses of your peer group, and the combination of a free Penguin and an extra half-a-crown a day 'jet' pay, certainly got right up their noses. I was happy.

Our Course settled in and after a fortnight's ground school we were split into two flights, half to fly in the mornings, the other half in the afternoons with the afternoon teams getting the morning slot the next day. Sixteen of us started but only eleven finished with the other five being 'washed out' at various times over the nine months. Reasons varied from failing to go solo, air sickness, lack of ability or, later on, from lack of ability to fly on instruments – a very important jet requirement. On the last day of our ground school, before flying started, we went to get our 'jet pilot' bone domes; lesser pilots who flew Piston Provosts did not merit these. I took mine back to the mess and spent the weekend painting it a glossy pillar box red with a black Ace of Spades emblem on each side, on the grounds that if you are going to be an ace you might as well let everyone know. Oh dear! Monday morning, an address from our flight commander. He started off by saying "Now you have all got your bone domes I want to make it quite clear that I do not want anyone painting theirs under any circumstances". The cold hand of fear clawed at my stomach: I saw him afterwards, owned up, showed him what I had done and was allowed to keep it throughout my training. We were introduced to our instructors – mine was Flt. Sgt. 'Jock' Naismith, although I naturally called him Sir, and thought he was just the best guy in the world. My life's dream was about to start. It was July 19th 1956.

The RAF in the 1950s was clearly descended from that of the 1930s, which in turn had obvious army origins. The days started with colour hoisting parades. Wednesday afternoons were sports days, Saturday mornings were station parades and the whole station stopped for lunch every day, and then slowly wound up at two, until closing for tea at five o'clock. All very military, English, ordered and correct. It was assumed that no other ranks had bank accounts and they had to attend a pay parade and have it handed out in cash; officers, and we were all now 'Acting Pilot Officers' were paid by the banking system. No one can describe me as a 'bleeding heart liberal' and that dreadful American term 'politically correct' had not been invented, even in America, but I was always surprised when we had a full station parade, taken by the Station Commander himself, to hear the Padre being introduced, followed by the command 'Fall Out Roman Catholics and Jews'. At this point half a dozen sheepish individuals would 'fall out', march off the parade ground and stand 'at ease'. The Padre (Anglican of course) would then say a short prayer, we would then say 'Amen' and the 'Fall In Roman Catholics and Jews' would be given; the same half a dozen sheepish individuals would then march back to their places and the parade would continue.

At last however we started flying. I loved it but had not realised how many cockpit drills had to be performed for each flight – it had just not crossed my mind. There were external checks, pre-start checks, after start checks, pre take off checks, checks during take off, after take off checks, fuel checks (all the time), pre aerobatic checks, returning to base checks, down wind checks, finals checks and shut down checks. I loved the flying but practically reduced my poor instructor to tears over all these checks, or rather my lack of ability to remember them; fifty years later as a Jet Provost instructor myself (unpaid) I realise that we needed a simulator or cockpit drill trainer. It was very difficult to find an empty cockpit to practice drills, as the aircraft were either flying, being turned round between flights or worked on in the hangars. Whichever it was the last thing that was needed was sixteen students each trying to find an empty cockpit to practise all the endless checks.

Royal Air Force Hullavington was a small 1930s station with a huge and excellent mess; the runways were a little short and the jets a little faster in the circuit than the Piston Provosts, so we went to a disused airfield at Keevil, twenty miles south of Hullavington, for our circuit work. After I had done about five hours we were flying circuits at Keevil and I had just done a perfectly reasonable landing when the aircraft shuddered and the right wing dropped most alarmingly. Jock Naismith took over control, slammed the engine to full power, raised the wing and took off again just before we cartwheeled; the right hand undercarriage leg had snapped so we flew back to Hullavington, burnt off most of our fuel and landed with one hanging down and two up. The aircraft landed and stopped, with the cockpit full of smoke, in a couple of hundred yards. I unstrapped, leaped out and ran but Jock Naismith was a long way ahead of me. He had grown up with Spitfires and petrol and knew what petrol could do. Paraffin was much safer but his instincts had been well honed. Our undercarriage leg had fractured right at the top from metal fatigue, the crystalline structure being clearly visible; fatigue had been induced as we had been flying from the grass strip beside the hard runway and from then on no further grass landings were made. The long undercarriage legs were fine on runways but could not take a grass strip however smooth it appeared to be.

My wheels up landing was my only excitement during my training.

However, two of our jet engines flamed out and then failed to start again while flying aerobatics; as a result we had to complete our course without any inverted flight until the last week or two. Both the aircraft landed wheels up in the countryside with very little damage and both were quickly repaired and returned to us. Only a year or two later no pilot would have landed wheels up away from home as the RAF had become addicted to its, far more dangerous, ejection seats.

It was a glorious summer – in retrospect they all are - and my circuits at Keevil were improving slowly. Sometimes we would do a full stop landing and taxi round the airfield past the control tower. Jock Naismith was very keen on cricket and one of the ATC staff would pop out of the tower with a blackboard and the latest test score. And then one glorious day, 31st July 1956 to be precise, Jock climbed out and sent me solo. I experienced no joy, no freedom of the skies feeling, all I could remember after landing, was a desperate rush to get one lot of checks done before I had to start the next lot. Facts were facts, however, and I was a pilot, better still a jet pilot, and I was eighteen and a half.

Most of the other pilots went solo fairly quickly. Chris Gould could be seen climbing out of the cockpit clutching a sick bag, even when flying solo, but by persevering he overcame his sickness, stayed in the RAF, and became a Group Captain. Shortly after I went solo I nearly had a serious crash entirely due to my own fault; I had touched down far too fast, 120 knots to be exact, against the 85 knots book figure. There was no way I could have stopped so, quite correctly, I decided to go round and land again – quite incorrectly I reached forward and retracted the undercarriage before applying power, the aircraft then sank to the ground still just flying and settled in 'ground effect'. I then, almost too late, opened the throttle and discovered that it takes a very long time to develop thrust in a jet engine; I didn't know how long eight seconds could be. Meanwhile I was flying down the airfield two or three feet from the ground and with my hand locked solid in terror on the control column. Having flown two thirds of the runway at a terrifyingly low height, power developed and I climbed ahead and then turned down wind to land safely. The story was not quite over. "Haig-Thomas, the Flight Commander wants to see you." I knew I was finished after such an appallingly dangerous mistake – luck was with me, however. I got a monumental rocket for low flying down the runway finishing with the immortal words "Even I could not fly that low and if I ever see anything like it again you will be out". I had got away with it and have never flown that low again since, nobody could.

My love life seemed to be suffering; in fact it didn't exist. All the other students on the course were coming back from weekends with tales of action that would have done credit to Casanova; and then it dawned on me that I needed a car. With a car any girl could be mine just for the asking. Not far outside Hullavington was a garage that sold cars and for £40 a Morris four seater that had left the factory twenty years earlier was mine. I had driven the family Land Rover at home, under instruction from my mother, and anyway I was a jet pilot – driving would come naturally – so away I went minus £40 with no tax, no licence and certainly no insurance. To possess these simply had not occurred to me. For a couple of months I drove happily round Wiltshire looking for young unattached beauties with no luck; once I stalled at the traffic lights in Chippenham and the car would not start, but two policemen walked across and gave me a push-start, never querying the absence of a tax disc or my qualifications. Those were the days. Don Betts was the grandfather on No.120 (not forgetting the Jet) Course; he was twenty-five, married and had a Triumph two seat roadster. When he heard of my legal status he made me get some insurance and tax, but I still had no licence. Shortly afterwards I read that the cost of a driving test was going to be £1, up from ten shillings, with effect from Monday. It was a Friday and, always careful with the pennies, I sent off my application with a cheque for ten shillings. I took the test in Bath and passed other than my ability to read a number plate at 25 yards. I explained that I was an RAF jet pilot with eyes like a hawk but was on a course of eye drops for a small and temporary eye infection. Satisfied, he ticked the boxes and at last I became a legal member of society four months after acquiring my mobile, but sadly unbaptised, love wagon.

John Butterley – always known as 'Stack'- was a great character. He introduced me to Bill Haley and his Comets and, even today, if I hear 'Rock Around The Clock' I am transported back to Hullavington and the emergent youth that we all were in 1956. Another favourite was Lonnie Donnegan and his skiffle group with 'Rock Island Line' and songs about the legendary train driver Casey Jones. Stack's love life had hit a bad patch as well so we set off for the nurses' training college in Bath where they had a dance every Saturday night. The love wagon was washed and we departed with high hopes. The master plan was to choose our girls, get them drunk and then – well, who knows? The plan went right on schedule until the object of my affections got so drunk that she was taken back to her rooms by her fellow students and, by eleven o'clock, Stack and I were back at Hullavington boasting of our easy conquests.

Apart from flame out landings in open country and my 'wheels up' landing there were very few incidents during our time at Hullavington; a piston Provost landing at night bounced its wheels on top of a bus and a Hunter, desperately short of fuel, landed on one of our short runways. This caused a huge amount of excitement; the pilot was on his first solo and deserved a great pat on the back for stopping the aircraft on such a short runway but not quite so much praise when he remained locked in the cockpit having forgotten how to open it and, missing a set of pilots notes, could not do so. Hullavington was also a maintenance unit and there were four or five hangars on the far side of the airfield packed with Avro Lincolns and de Havilland Mosquitos. The Mossies were brand new having flown in from the factory to storage as, apparently, it had been cheaper to let the contract run off than to pay the penalties for early termination. Those beautiful aircraft were pushed out of the hangar; the Merlin engines were cut off and then the engine-less aircraft pushed back to be burned; even then it seemedcomplete sacrilege.

The RAF training regime is designed to be very demanding with a few hours devoted to all the flight exercises that it is possible to do. Thus after going solo and consolidating, instrument flying, aerobatics, night flying, formation flying were all covered together with low level map reading and high level radio cross countries. Just as one could relax and enjoy some particular aspect of flight one started again on another one; to me night flying was complete heaven and totally removed from anything else. It is one of my regrets that I always did so little as it was not a major feature of life in the day fighter role when I eventually got my wings. The end of the course came; we had lost five of our number washed out over nine months. I flew my last flight with Jock Naismith on February 22nd 1957. I was now just nineteen, had 96 hours and 15 minutes total flying time and our course was posted to No.8 Advanced Flying School for the next phase of our training on de Havilland Vampires. I packed up the, by now very inappropriately named, love wagon and headed for some leave. Driving home I began to realise that, compared with nine months ago, my 'ace' status, achieved before I started flying, needed down grading to just exceptional!

Chapter 4

VAMPIRES

Our Course left Hullavington at the end of February 1957. I could take off and land, fly in cloud, fly in formation, perform basic aerobatics and, my favourite, fly at night. I packed up the love wagon and set off for a fortnight's leave at the parental home near Harwich; driving out of London in the dark I had to get out to see if my headlights were on – they were. No MOT tests in those days! During my leave I arranged to lunch with an old school friend, Andrew Rodwell, and my first cousin, Lindsay Bury and set off in the LW. I put the hood down to make it feel more like a 'straight eight' Bentley tourer from the 1930s. Lindsay and I donned our overcoats, as in those days February was actually very cold, and away we went. I have always driven fast but speed was not the LW's strong suit. However, rounding a right hand bend at a foot on the floor maximum flat out 48mph, she generated sufficient lateral 'g' for the passenger door to fly open and to this day I can still see in my rear mirror my cousin rolling down the road in his overcoat like a huge tennis ball. Mercifully he was unhurt, bar a few grazes, but I began to wonder if I should trade in this, definitely past its best, machine. Not only was it falling apart but it didn't seem to attract the girls that I had hoped for, so I sold it for £10, borrowed £100 from my parents and bought a beautifully restored Morris 8 two seater of 1932 vintage and capable of 45mph flat out. With this car and my own natural handsome profile, I expected to have more girls than I could handle; well, at least one would be nice.

Our leave was soon over and my new car and I arrived at Royal Air Force Swinderby to rejoin the rest of my course, or those that had not been 'scrubbed' on Jet Provosts. We were to fly de Havilland Vampires with dual in the awful T.11 two seat side by side version followed by solo flying in the heavenly single seat Mk V version which was not only wonderful to fly but, best of all, had been retired from real Fighter Squadrons and some of them were still camouflaged. Swinderby was a hutted camp half way between Newark and Lincoln; during the war it had been a heavy bomber conversion unit but it had lots of hangars and, I guess, probably eighty Vampires in total. The Vampire was powered by a de Havilland Goblin engine with 3500lbs of thrust twice the power of our Viper engined Jet Provosts. The Goblin engines centrifugal compressor produced a wonderful wailing noise that, when I hear it today, takes me back in time just as much as Bill Haley's 'Rock Around The Clock' does. I could never understand why the Goblin wailed so distinctively when the very similar centrifugal compressors of the Rolls Royce Derwents and Nenes made just a smooth whistling sound. We were introduced to our instructors; mine was 'Pete' Adair - 'Sir' to me - and he had been on a Meteor day fighter Squadron. There was a lot of one upmanship amongst the students to have a fighter pilot instructor and I felt even more superior to have one of my own.

The advanced flying course was largely a repeat of the Jet Provost course but with the addition of our first nibble at the effects of the speed of sound on subsonic aircraft as. With its extra thrust, Sir Geoffrey's blood sucking mammal could easily attain 35000', and if one had time, 40,000' could appear as another magical number on the altimeter. The Advanced Flying School training was again half ground school and half flying but, with our JP backgrounds, none of us had any trouble flying the aircraft although the air force still made us do nine or ten trips each before going solo.

So far during our training the grim reaper had stayed away from Hullavington but during our time at Swinderby he arrived and took two students and one instructor. The instructor was David Kirkup who was posted to us from a Shackleton Squadron; naturally no one wanted a heavy aircraft instructor and no one was to have him as it turned out. Our Flight Commander, Stan Sollitt, decided that the new instructor needed more formation flying before flying with us as an instructor and he was No.3 in a Vic of Vampires. The formation climbed through cloud with an instructor leading, John Blount as No.2 on the right, and DK No.3 on the left. His formation flying was very rough and, descending back through cloud, his aircraft lost the formation, reappeared banked straight at the leader followed by a rapid reversal away from it. When the formation broke through the cloud base there was a grim black pillar of smoke where DK's Vampire had crashed after failing to transition to instrument flight. No one seemed particularly concerned, but flying was cancelled for our course for one afternoon as the instructors all went to his funeral.

The Vampire was capable of climbing to height in a perfectly tolerable time and here we were introduced to the mysteries of 'the sound barrier' and why it was thus named. As subsonic aircraft approach Mach unity, shock waves form on lumps and bumps as localised airflow becomes temporarily supersonic and this leads to a breakdown of the airflow behind the shock wave. If a wave forms on one wing that wing will drop temporarily as it loses lift relative to the other; things get more exciting however if the shock wave destroys the airflow over the tailplane. An aircraft is stable in pitch because there is a permanent down load on the tail – if, however, this download is suddenly reduced the aircraft will pitch nose down very violently, the high Mach number will be maintained and pulling back on the stick will have very little effect if the elevators are blanketed behind the shock wave. The point of this elementary lesson in transonic aerodynamics is that there had been another fatal accident. A student pilot had died in his single seat Vampire in a steep straight dive into the Lincolnshire countryside and it was thought that corrugations, which were certainly present on the tailplanes of all the single seaters, might have been the source of multiple shock waves that triggered the dive and then, by leaving the elevators in disturbed airflow, prevented recovery. One of our instructors was Master Pilot Evans and he was given the task of doing a 'Mach run' in every single seat Vampire at Swinderby to see if he could replicate the situation, but no problem was encountered. The whole hypothesis was improbable because if control is lost at high level extending the airbrakes and reducing power will cure the whole unpleasantness as thicker air is encountered at around 15000'. Much the most likely cause was a lack of oxygen by the pilot, then known as anoxia, but now called hypoxia. It is easy now to criticise but in 1957 it was only ten years since the legendary Yeager had become the first man to exceed Mach One in an aircraft and none of our instructors had flown supersonic. So we climbed our Vampires and snaked and pitched and flicked and landed and wrote 'EX31 High Speed Run' in our logbooks. I loved that bit.

Shortly after the start of our flying at Swinderby the Minister of Defence,

Duncan Sandys, stood up in the House of Commons to announce a new Defence White Paper. The principle part of this paper was to declare that manned fighter aircraft were a thing of the past and, from now on, air defence would be conducted by missiles; he was quite right about that but wrong in that he thought the missiles would be on the ground whereas in fact they would be air launched from air superiority fighters. I failed to grasp the significance of this new defence policy and its impact on my life plan. Very shortly afterwards, however, it became clear as all the auxiliary Fighter Squadrons were disbanded together with most of the 2nd Tactical Air Force Squadrons in Germany, and a great swathe of the UK air defence squadrons in the home based Fighter Command. Worst of all the disastrous effect was felt immediately at Swinderby as there were no postings to the Hunter Conversion units at all and the whole RAF was awash with fighter pilots who had nothing to do. We had six months training left to get our wings and during that time there were no fighter postings and all graduating pilots were sent Transport Command to fly four engined Beverleys or Hastings with no opportunity to bag a couple of MIG-15s before breakfast. Things were bad.

We all do things we are ashamed of with hindsight and even I am no exception. One day there was a full station parade - I overslept and consequently missed it. I had breakfast with one other student from another course in an otherwise empty mess and went down to 'the flights' full of trepidation. No one had missed me. There were two more parades scheduled so I did a tactical oversleep and still no one missed me. The parades were in anticipation of the AOC's annual inspection and there was a full dress rehearsal, one which even I thought that I should attend. When I arrived I found that I was in 'battle dress', our everyday uniform, but everyone else was in 'best blue' No.1 Service Dress. There were however a few national service pilots who did not have a No.1 SD. First of all there was a roll call (for the first time) and then, during the inspection, names were taken of the national service pilots who, because I was attired like them, erroneously included me and we were then excused all further parades. This did not make me very popular with the rest of my course as I wandered in on parade days having enjoyed a lengthy breakfast and the morning papers while they practiced march-pasts and all the various drills that are laid on for visiting Air Marshals.

The other student pilot that I had breakfasted with on that first occasion with the genuine oversleep took off in a Vampire 5 later that day and flew into a thunderstorm near Gainsborough. His aircraft broke up and an elderly couple, hearing a crash from upstairs, found a hole in their roof and his body in their bath. A little later the Mae West he had been wearing turned up, allocated to our squadron, complete with some bloodstains on it. Parsimony with the taxpayers assets is to be commended but Stan Sollitt had it sent back to the safety equipment section together with some of the very succinct phraseology for which he was well known.

Our flying continued without incident. I had a problem with my instrument flying, or to be more specific with steep turns on limited panel, which involved three extra sorties; I loved the night flying and felt from my little cockpit with the glowing instruments and the quiet hum of the engine that I was alone in the centre of the universe. Perversely, as I was eventually to spend my air force career in the single seat world, I was to do very little flying in the dark – had I done more, perhaps the novelty would have worn off; I doubt it. One high level exercise that we flew could only be done in a Vampire and I know of no other jet that could fly it, a very high level loop. The aim was to start at Mach .82, a whisper below the .84 at which the aircraft would, typically, start porpoising, and a height of 30,000'. The aircraft was then inched into a climb, anything other than a very slight pitch input would cause it to enter a compressibility stall and start to flick. Very slowly, as the aircraft pitched up, increasing amounts of stick input could be applied until, if you were lucky, the little Vampire would fly over the top at close to 40,000' with no airspeed, a ballistic trajectory, and full power from the Goblin producing around a quarter of its sea level thrust. Any rough handling at any point during this manoeuvre would initiate a series of violent auto-rotational flicks; Jim Baldwin lost it on one flight and said that his aircraft had flicked up to 42,000' before it fell off in a spin. Easy to see why this exercise was only flown dual.

I flew one sortie which, now being much older and wiser, I wish that I had not, but as a teenager one's judgment on such matters is never good. I had a session of solo aerobatics scheduled and the weather forecast was for a glorious summer day - which can happen in England from time to time - so I decided that it was time for my parents and sibling sisters and brothers to see just what an ace their son and big brother had become after only a year's experience - not to mention the 150 hours total time in his logbook. I spent the night before with my maps and pilots notes and found that I could take off from Lincoln, climb to 30,000', let down, give the family a 'beat up' and make it back to Swinderby via another 30,000' climb. This is the classic and only way to fly a long-range strike in 1950s aircraft, although I did not know this at the time. The flight went as planned, the family lived on a little island near Harwich so there were no complaints and my sisters said that there was a horrid smell of paraffin after I had flown past. Clear evidence of success.

About two thirds of the way through our advanced flying school course I became seriously worried about the complete block on the recruitment of fighter pilots; I had had a tremendous battle to get into the RAF with my appalling eyesight (6/9 6/12, with astigmatism, for those of a technical disposition) and now another fight was looming. It seemed impossible for the air force to block all recruitment forever so I embarked on a sustained campaign on the simple principle of nothing venture, nothing gain. One of the exercises that accompanied formation flying was 'tail chasing' where the two formating aircraft followed the leader round the sky holding a constant 200-300 yards behind him solely by manoeuvring flight. If you were too close you allowed your aircraft to slide a little to the outside of a turn and vice versa; it could be very hard work, especially when dual, as the T11 had ejection seats in a very small cockpit and the resultant upright posture is very uncomfortable when under sustained G. Whenever I flew dual tail chase I used to fly as aggressively as possible and intersperse my grunts, greying vision and slight feelings of sickness with remarks such as 'Now we've got him, Sir, if only we had guns!' and other what now seem like rather immature comments. In short I made it clear that air combat manoeuvring was right up my street. My next opportunity came nearer the end of our Course; I had committed some crime and been sentenced by Stan Sollitt to clean and tidy the Squadron Commander's office. I swept it out, emptied the ashtrays and waste paper basket and then had a brain wave when I saw the blotting paper pad that was on all desks in those days, much as computers are now. I removed the top piece of much used blotting paper and replaced it with a virgin white new piece, then, finding a red pen I wrote neatly in the top left hand corner 'Memo – get Hunter posting for Pilot Officer Haig-Thomas'. I said nothing, he said nothing. Finally, just before the Course ended, and following Stan Sollitt's discovery that I was wearing a very tasteful dark maroon pair of socks with my uniform, I was sentenced to write out twenty five times why I was improperly dressed. I wrote neatly that 'I was wearing red socks with my uniform as my black ones had been sent on to RAF Chivenor in anticipation of my Hunter conversion there'. Then I went to Station Head Quarters where a very helpful young WAAF 'Roneo'd' me twenty-five copies and the next day I placed these on Stan's desk. Again nothing was said but no Hunter postings went to the Course in front of us after their graduation so my prospects were not good.

The day before our 'Wings' parade I stood outside our flight offices with my instructor and Stan Sollitt when there was a mighty roar and a Gloster Javelin two seat night fighter with a huge Delta shaped wing appeared from behind the hangars during an overshoot from a low approach. "That will be Pete Poppy," said Stan as the earth trembled with power. "He used to instruct on our flight and he is just trying to piss me off." I went weak in the knees with admiration, desire and jealousy.

Our passing out parade came and went; it was my first touch from an Air Marshal as he pinned the wings on my breast. I stepped back and saluted after which we were meant to turn left and march off. I ended up left all right but through nerves, only after having turned right through 270°, a manoeuvre that is not easy and certainly not in the drill books. Terror and awe in the presence of God had blown my mind but no one seemed to notice, to my great relief. We had a dining out night for our Course and I got drunk, not just tipsy but drunk; I never made the dinner and was helped back to my room by Andy Pryde and Graham Clements and then I was ill, very ill, all night. I was still ill the next morning and arrived very late at the Squadron where I was told never to let it happen again - and I never have! I have always had a very low tolerance for alcohol and am well on the way before others have even started - it was a lesson well learned.

Our Course was sent en bloc to Valley on Anglesey in North Wales where we would await our postings and where we could stay in flying practice with the occasional Vampire flight. I was very proud to have my wings and very worried about my future. I packed up my now faithful little Morris 8. We had clocked many miles together round the teachers training colleges looking for love or something like it and PO 9513 was well known at Lincoln, Retford and Doncaster Ladies Training Colleges for teachers. I can still remember the telephone number for Doncaster – it was Mexborough 2159 but as I am now nearly seventy, I am afraid it will do me little good.

Chapter 5

VALLEY & CHIVENOR

Royal Air Force Valley is on the North West corner of Anglesey and has a wild atmosphere about it, surrounded as it is by sea with great long beaches and as far from civilisation as one can get. Alas Valley also had wartime huts, but we were used to these from Swinderby and in any case with our wings on our left breast and our left breasts thrust well forward for all to see, who cared. Pilots in all air forces have wings but the RAF ones are a wonderful design, they are big and white so no one can miss them and at twice the size of those worn by lesser mortals such as navigators.

Our Course arrived at this coastal heaven just after Christmas 1957, and on December 31st, I started flying the Vampire again as there was a training squadron there to keep newly qualified ex-students in current flying practice until our postings came through. Also at Valley was the Guided Weapons Development Unit flying Swift F.7s; they had half a dozen Swifts with beautiful long noses and an afterburner at the rear. They were flown by four test pilots who kept themselves to themselves and, in their late twenties, were as old as God. They defied all my attempts to lure them into tales of derring-do and terrifying experiences and did not seem very keen to hear about mine. One day, as I walked back from our flight hut there was a Swift in the circuit; I was passing the end of the runway along the beach back to the mess and stopped right on the threshold to watch. The Swift came round finals with everything extended for landing and then the power came on and the pilot lit the 'burner right over my head as he took the aircraft round for another approach. The noise and power were indeed awesome and having stayed to watch his final landing, I continued back to the mess weak at the knees with longing. I just had to fly fighters.

Just before we had arrived at Valley the Navy had left, or, to be more accurate, were leaving as a few tail enders remained. A reminder of the hazards of young men in fighters was on a Queen Mary trailer near the mess; it was a Sea Hawk. The pilot, having gained his wings at Valley had been flying Sea Hawks at Lossiemouth and had returned to Valley on a cross-country. Apparently he had done a very fast join and break into the Valley pattern followed by an exceptionally tight circuit during which he stalled the aircraft, crashed and was killed. I made a mental note to avoid very tight circuits.

And then one day it happened – our postings came through. We had been the second all jet-trained Course and, logically, should fly jets, not because of our great jet flying abilities but because we knew nothing about piston engine technology. The Air Force however was still awash with jet pilots in ground jobs after the great '57 White Paper with its 'no more manned fighters after the Lightning and precious few of these' policy. Eleven of us out of the sixteen that started finally wore our wings and of these Jim Baldwin and Don Betts were sent to fly Canberras, the rest were split between Transport Command Beverleys and Coastal Command Shackletons. Fighter Command, however, wanted a trickle of young pilots to fly Hunters and it was to RAF Chivenor, near Barnstaple in Devon, that I was posted to fly the glorious Hunter. I packed up my little Morris two seater and drove for twelve hours at a maximum of 42 mph stopping twice for petrol, and once for a puncture, until I arrived home for a long weekend before driving to Chivenor. It amazes me now that very long drives were done in those days with no radio and no heater and yet I was never bored; the countryside was still countryside, there was very little traffic, lorries were limited to 20mph and, to all intents and purposes, there were no dual carriageways – not that I was in a position to overtake anything anyway. During my leave I fell in love – she was very young but then so was I, so at least we had something in common.

I could hardly wait to get to Chivenor and at the beginning of March 1958 the Morris and I set off for Devon on another epic drive and, on arriving at Chivenor, found yet another hutted encampment by the lovely Tor estuary. There were six of us on my Course, two others from other training schools and the rest on short courses run to refamiliarise or convert Wing Commanders Flying and Squadron Commanders designate.

The Hunter conversion course in 1958 was simple short and safe; there were no two-seaters in those days so if you were twenty years old with two hundred hours in your logbook the Hunter was an exciting ride. The first fortnight was spent on learning the aircraft systems and numbers with numerous trips in the simulators. Then we went to fly, first two Vampire T.11 sorties to check instrument proficiency and learn the area's principle geographical features with an instructor, then one solo trip still in the Vampire. Presumably this was to give a little confidence to the students that they could still fly by themselves. Confidence was needed because the Hunter was a quantum leap in performance and engineering over the Vampire; it had a best rate of climb speed of 420 knots against 240 for the Vampire, it had powered controls, it was supersonic and it looked like heaven.

The simulators were quite astonishingly good considering that fifties electronics were very primitive, and they provided an almost perfect facsimile of flying a Hunter in cloud but with no relative motion. The simulator instructors were part of the flotsam and jetsam of the Duncan Sandys tsunami; good young individuals whose lives had been blighted by a policy change in Whitehall through no fault of their own. Unfortunately, for students like me, they had morphed into complete bastards who would have regarded the Marquis de Sade as a rank amateur - at least that was my perception as I flew simulator sorties under an ever increasing series of sequential, cumulative, and improbable emergencies. The instructor would sit at his console and I would sit in the cockpit with the hood shut and all the needles 'on the numbers' climbing 'in cloud' on, for example, a high level cross country. The instructor would then fail one system after another giving an ever-increasing workload to the pilot until he ejected or landed back at Chivenor, a very rare occurrence. If you ejected too early you were clearly unsuitable material to be entrusted with one of Her Majesty's shiny new fighters. If you ejected too late you had wasted the money spent training you only to die when you could have lived. The effect of simulator flight was total reality on the human mind and I would finish each session soaked in sweat and mentally exhausted. What it ultimately meant was that if a real failure occurred, any student pilot could cope with it automatically. Flight simulators were wonderful and the best possible value the air force could have had from its investment – whatever they cost.

And then it happened. On March 13th 1958 I flew the solo Vampire sortie and, after lunch, my first solo in the Hunter – with, I might add, considerable apprehension. I was to take off, climb to 20,000' (about two minutes) conduct some general handling, let down to 11,000' and fly a pretend circuit and landing with 'touch down' at 10,000'; after which I was to rejoin the circuit and land. I walked out to the aircraft with an instructor, wishing for the first time that I had been specially selected for transport aircraft. Having strapped in, started up, and conducted all my pre-take off drills under the watchful supervision of the instructor, he gave me a pat on the shoulder and mouthed the words 'good luck'. I was on my own and wishing it wasn't March 13th. The Hunter's brakes were very effective and the undercarriage gave a fairly hard ride as I taxied out to Chivenor's 27 runway. As I rolled past the Officers' Mess I remembered how I had laughed at the story of an Iraqi student who, when he arrived at the point where I was, had put on the brakes, climbed out of his Hunter leaving the engine running, and was eventually found sitting in the Officers' Mess reading a paper and refusing to admit that he had ever been in the aircraft. As a solution to my own apprehension it somehow didn't seem very British. I lined up, opened up the engine, and let the brakes off. The beast surged forward like a cannon shot; I raised the nose at 120 knots (the poor little Vampire left the ground at 105) and was airborne at 150. Imagine, if you can, trying to balance two razor blades one on top of the other edge to edge, a small aileron input to raise a wing resulted in the other one going down 20°, picking that up merely reversed the situation. I disappeared from the airfield rocking my wings like all first solo pilots and then, a little late, I raised the undercarriage and flaps. The Hunter soared upwards and I noticed 7000' already on the altimeter. I hadn't crashed yet.

Very soon I was at 25,000' sitting in silence in a little private bubble; the sun shone, the sky was blue and out to the west I could see Lundy Island. Moving my wrist to the left the Hunter spun at its full 270° a second; I pulled a little G and got smacked hard by the G-suit which I had forgotten about. Another roll and a timid wingover – I could almost be enjoying myself if at the back of my mind hadn't niggled the fact that I had to land, and soon. The Mach meter read .9, the fuel gauges 2000lbs. I popped the airbrakes out and slid down to 11,000' to do a practice circuit. The flaps went down 2 and then 4 clicks at 300 kts followed by the undercarriage; I was now over Hartland Point and heading west. I rolled on the bank and, at 180 kts, came round my imaginary final turn to land on my imaginary runway at 10,000'. I completed the turn and found that I was at 7000' or, to put it another way, 3000' underground. Not very reassuring.

I called the tower that I was at Barnstaple for a rejoin, ran up the field, turned down wind dropping flaps, retracting airbrakes and, finally, to make the landing smoother pushed the down button on the undercarriage. In the Hunter the runway threshold had to be crossed at 135kts about 5' to 10' off the ground; the numbers came up, the Hunter landed on hard, I lowered the nose and braked as firmly as I dared. I was down; I was safe; the aircraft was in one piece and I could have jumped over the moon with happiness and pride. I shut down the engine and, after climbing down the ladder, could hardly breathe, surviving only with little tiny short breaths. This was actually quite normal and was caused by the pressure from the G-suit partially collapsing the pilots lungs when fed with 100% oxygen. After two or three minutes of breathlessness my lungs re-inflated and normal functions returned. Everything had happened so quickly that I had not really had time to enjoy it. The fuel burn was astronomic as after 30 minutes I was down to landing fuel which was 10 minutes before the engine said goodnight. My aircraft was a Hunter F.4 which had much more fuel than the Hunter F.1 where average high level sorties were 20 to 25 minutes whereas in the F.4 we averaged 40 minutes. That evening I wrote up my log book: 'March 13th. Hunter F.4. convex-one. First solo on type; 35 minutes'. We had a short period of bad weather and then in four days I flew a further 10 sorties, covering most of the flight envelope in which we would normally operate in. I flew to 45,000'; I flew in manual control where the controls appeared to be set in concrete; I flew radar approaches off a QGH let down and finally, of course, I flew supersonic.

In the 1980s I flew at Mach 2 in Concorde out of New York and ordered another portion of Lobster Thermidor and a top up to my glass of Dom Perignon but in the 1950s flying 'through the sound barrier' was derring-do. According to the films, controls reversed (they didn't), pilots died (they did, but not from supersonic flight) and only supermen could do it – at least they got that bit right. It is difficult to comprehend now but in 1957 it was only ten years since Chuck Yeager had exceeded Mach unity and that had been in a rocket ship however most of the 1950's jets showed very undesirable flight characteristics in both roll and pitch between M.78 and .84 or in any manoeuvre close to those numbers. The Hunter did not, they said, even beyond M1.0. March 19th and Convex 6. I tucked the wheels up and soared heavenwards, no wing rock on take off, and my thinking processes at last up to speed with the aircraft. I climbed out to the west under control from Hartland radar to my briefed 45,000'; it was a glorious cold crisp day. Lundy Island lay behind me and the moment had come. I called Hartland for clearance for a 'Boom run', so named after the big double boom generated by an aircraft in supersonic flight. Hartland cleared me and, feeling a little apprehensive, I rolled the Hunter inverted, pulled the nose down into an appropriately steep dive and rolled out level. The Mach meter slid up towards .96 .97 .98 and there it stopped; what a humiliation. I used the main tail trim to recover, as elevators are pretty ineffective at high Mach numbers, got crushed by my G-suit, and climbed back to 45,000'. Hartland cleared me for a second run and this time I went for it pulling the nose right down before rolling out. The Mach meter paused and went to 1.05. Inside the aircraft nothing happened, other than the magic number and a quick rudder movement on the pedals as the shockwave passed the hinge line on the rudder. I returned to Chivenor and felt as if I had lost my virginity again – something the love of my life had yet to experience in her life but no doubt the weekend coming would change all that. No girl would be able to resist hearing at first hand, several times over, what it was like to break the sound barrier.

A week after my first solo my conversion flying was over. The air force operate weapons systems not expensive toys, the only purpose of the Hunters that I was flying was to shoot down Russian bombers and so the rest of the course was devoted to tactical formation flying, use of the gunsight and finally the guns. I also realised that I was now in the RAF proper. During our training we had been treated like school children, and as most of us had only just left school that seemed quite reasonable. Here at Chivenor there were no parades, no ground school just flying, actually not just flying but the world's best flying in the world's best looking aircraft. One small problem remained which was lunch – pilots could not have it. Getting dressed to fly was a complex business, first on went a pair of 'long johns' on top of these went the zipped up G suit and then there was a five minute struggle to get into an immersion suit. Once in there was no way one would take it all off and then put it all back on just for lunch and pilots were not allowed in the mess in their flying kit so – no lunch. Eventually this was changed and a room was set aside for the students, a little group of lepers in their flying kit in the tradesmen's quarters, while the full glory of the mess proper was reserved for the non pilots.

One day the Wing Commander Flying cancelled all flying and made everyone return to their Squadrons from the main briefing (held every morning like a school assembly), put on all flying kit and wait. Buses eventually turned up and all the 229 OCU students and instructors were taken out in two Air Sea Rescue launches into the cold Atlantic waters near Hartland Point. Everyone was then made to jump into the sea, inflate their dinghies and wait to be picked up by the Chivenor helicopter. For two hours we waited until rescue came; some pilots were very cold as they had stretched the neck and wrist seals on their immersion suits which, filled with water, were then deprived of their insulating properties. Wing Commander Flying had noticed this undesirable suit stretching and varied the dinghy drill from the usual jump in and get rescued, to jump in, wait for two hours, get very cold indeed, and then get rescued. Another lesson learned. There was one rather odd occurrence when Wing Commander Admin left very suddenly. Apparently, finding the Hunter rather alarming and being obliged to do so many hours a year, he had filled his logbook with fictitious flights and, when he put it to the Group Captain for signature, the alert 'Groupie' noticed that he had been flying on dates when he knew that the Wing Commander had been away. At the time I was contemptuous but now I am more sympathetic; first of all there was no military need for this nearly retired man to fly this very expensive aircraft and, secondly, he would have learned to fly in 1930s biplanes. Then, probably having spent a very gallant war on bombers, he would have been quite unsuited temperamentally to ride a Hunter to the heavens. He would find the exercise, so easy for a young man, as difficult and daunting as I find my computer and for the same reason, inability to adapt in old age, i.e. in his case, his mid-forties.

The next part of the course was intended to turn us into fighter pilots, that is to say to use the aircraft as a weapon. A presumption is made at this juncture of a pilot's career that anyone who has got this far can take off, fly instruments, cope with emergencies, recover to base and land without running out of fuel, so the training was henceforward focussed on formation flying both close and tactical, and weapons work. There is no need to explain the technical difficulties of tactical formation flying with four aircraft. Close formation which is used for all take offs and climbs through cloud becomes second nature to any fast jet pilot. I found high level battle formation very demanding, but hugely satisfying, and operating every flight in formations of two or four infinitely more fun than taking off and flying solo which becomes boring quite quickly. I only had one excitement at Chivenor but that was quite enough. We had been briefed for a high level 'battle four' and climbed through a lot of cloud as two pairs, breaking out at 34,000' into a crystal blue. As soon as we were clear of cloud I moved to my No. 4 position on my section leader's left and then we joined up as a pair on the other two. Exercises began and all went well until I throttled back to idle, which makes little difference at that height and was just stupid; I then found my engine locked at idle. We were sixty odd miles from Chivenor with 30,000' of cloud between me and the ground and that cold hand of fear started to clutch at my heart. However many power failures a pilot has and I have now, at the time of writing had seven, the same gut tightening feeling grabs one. This was my first; I was a long way from home aged 20 with 250 hours total time and all that cloud between me and a runway. I forgot to say 'Mayday' etc and just called 'Blue leader, Blue four with engine failure turning for home'. I am forever grateful to Blue 3 whose name I forget, who slid into close formation on me just as I slipped into the grey mist at the top of the clouds. Completely useless but very comforting. We had been working Ventnor radar on the Isle of Wight and they gave me headings for Chivenor and handed us over to Hartland radar and thence Chivenor. On the way down I wished I had made my harnesses tighter and hoped that I had done my dinghy up properly. Our pair of Hunters arrived overhead base at around 8000' and when we popped out of cloud I was at the end of the down wind leg at 3000'. The Hunter sinks like a stone at slow speed with no power but I dumped the flaps and undercarriage and landed on runway 09. My engine was giving just enough power to taxi in and shut down. I climbed out very sweaty and failed to put in the ejection seat pins for which I got a bollocking and no one said, "Well done boy." The story does not quite end there because the engineers ground ran the engine and, finding nothing wrong, proclaimed it to be student finger trouble. The aircraft was given to an instructor for test and at 10,000' it went out completely instead of locking down at idling as it had for me. I was very pleased. He too 'dead sticked' it onto Chivenors 2000 yard runway but he was in manual control which is much tougher; at least my idling power kept the hydraulics on line.

On the north side of Chivenor was a small hangar and a flying club wherein resided one Maurice Looker, an Auster and a Miles Aerovan with which he hoped to fly services to Lundy Island. ML had been wartime RAF and had had a distinguished career with medals, which were not on view, but a classic RAF WWII handle bar moustache which certainly was. Sometime past, I mused, he too must have been like I was at a similar point in his life and for the first time I began to think of my economic future for this Maurice was a dreadful warning. Flying was the world's best job and flying the Hunter extra terrestrial but where did it lead? Not, I hoped, to a run down shack and an old Auster purporting to be a flying club.

Our course progressed from multiple aircraft high-level battle formations to ciné exercises with cameras on top of our gunsights. The leader would enter climbing diving and turning combinations while the student would expose endless reels of film under the title of ranging and tracking. Hitting another aircraft with bullets is actually quite difficult. The problem was worse with the 30mm cannon as it had a relatively low muzzle velocity and so any variation in range required a huge adjustment to compensate for either increased or decreased gravity drop. To start with I was not very good at it but like most things, if you learn them young enough you learn them quickly, and after not too many sorties, we went on the range, guns live, to see if we could hit an airborne target. As there were no dual control Hunters it was back to the trusty Vampire for dual air-to-air gunnery at a flag target towed by a Meteor.

This gunnery was academic; that is it was of no practical tactical use, and we flew what was known as a high quarter attack; the fighter flew parallel to the target 1500' above it with around half a mile lateral displacement. On turn-in the pilot lowered the nose, let the speed build and then reversed his turn aiming to be tracking the flag, which would be about 300 yards behind the Meteor, with a 30° angle off at 400 yards. Only one gun was fired and the bullets were all dipped in various paint colours so that on return the PAI (Pilot Attack Instructor) could count how many greens, reds or blue holes there were in the flag. It was also very competitive as you either had more holes than the other students or you did not; we had fifty rounds to fire in total from one gun and I have my scores in my log book 0.6.0.2.6.14. I loved it. The gunnery phase of the course brought me two interviews with one of the Weapons Instructors. At the first interview I had fired at a very low angle off from the flag; on my film, as I fired, were the flag and the towing Meteor. I was dispatched to the towing flight complete with my film to show the tug pilot how close he had come to death (not very). The second was occasioned after I had fired out on the flag and was returning to base when I had spotted Lundy Island. It seemed like a good idea to have on film what the ground looked like at 700mph. I wound up the Hunter and flew down Lundy filming as I went, at a perfectly legal height. The camera button and the gun trigger in the Hunter however were next to each other and as the PAI pointed out to me, when he chanced upon my film, I could have fired several rounds at the locals on Lundy. He was right of course – another stupidity.

And then our course was over. It had been quite staggeringly hard work and supremely satisfying. The atmosphere in the grown-up world was wonderfully relaxed. Chivenor, that Mecca for all Fighter Pilots in the 50s through to the late 70s, was just heaven on earth and anyone who went through the system always found it to be so. The grim reaper stayed away for the two months that we were there but the day we left a Wing Commander doing a refresher course after a ground appointment crashed two hundred yards short of runway 09 and was killed. Also, to show how times have changed, in those days terrorists had not been invented and anyone could drive in and out at Chivenor without being stopped; this even applied to insurance salesmen. There was one such named Bill Wrench-Buck, who spent a lot of time in our coffee bar selling insurance to young student fighter pilots, not, I would have thought, a recruiting ground likely to endear him to the underwriters. I was thinking of taking out a policy but then he told me that, on one course, he had sold policies to all six students and they were all dead. Being superstitious I thought that perhaps he had the evil eye so I declined and have never subsequently ever had life insurance.

There was one final act before I left Chivenor. My mentor instructor suggested that it would not be a good idea to arrive on my first Squadron with a glossy pillar-box red bonedome with a black ace of spades on it. It had served me well and was easy to find among all the silver ones, but I thought it good advice so went to the stores and changed it for a silver one. The first chapter of my life in the Air Force was over and it was time to go home and see if the love of my life had changed her mind. She hadn't.

Chapter 6

FIGHTER PILOT AT LAST

No.63(F) Sqn was based at Waterbeach just north of Cambridge. I loved that (F) bit. I had asked for a squadron that was East Anglian based and the RAF had listened and given me what I had asked for; it was midsummer, I was 20 and life could hardly be better. Well, it would have been a little better if, 'the love of my life' had tried to understand the problems and requirements of super human pilots who flew faster than sound.

Waterbeach was ten miles north of Cambridge. I had relations and school friends up at Trinity, and with a car I could go anywhere and park anywhere I wanted even right outside any shop or coffee bar that I wished to visit, something unthinkable today. The 'Beach' was home to three fighter squadrons, nos. 56 and 25 being the sister squadrons to No.63. Note the girlie adjective used to describe them. No. 56(F) Sqn flew Hunter 5s with Sapphire engines that, naturally, were less powerful than the 200 series Avons in our Hunter 6s, while 25(NF) Sqn flew long-nose Meteor Night Fighters, the NF.14. Finally there was the station flight with two Meteor F.8 single seat day fighters, recently retired from 63 Sqn, with an elderly Flight Lieutenant in charge, plus a Vampire and Meteor T.7 for training, on each of the day squadrons.

63 Sqn was commanded by Sqn Ldr 'Sid' Walker although I certainly did not call him 'Sid'; the two flights 'A' and 'B' were commanded by Mike Scarrott and Ken Appelboom respectively. I was on 'B' Flight but KA was on holiday so I went to see the 'A' Flight Commander instead. I went in to Mike Scarrott's office where he sat on a chair behind a desk in an otherwise empty room – no pictures, no files, and no books. "You the new pilot are you?" he began, and when I replied in the affirmative, he continued "I have one piece of advice that I give to all new pilots and it is this - if your hair starts falling out, or you are not getting it regularly, then get married; otherwise don't". I stood there absorbing this deep philosophical concept for life. "Why are you standing there, what do you want?" "I hoped to fly, sir." "I will get Mike Davis to give you a sector recce – MIKE." Through the

door came Mike Davis looking just like a fighter pilot ought to look but with a large hooked nose, everyone called him 'Hooky' Davis but never to his face. "Give this lad a look round the local area in the Meteor will you, but before you do tell those bastards who stripped my office bare to bring it all back." Mike was a Flying Officer, well overdue for promotion, who had never taken his promotion exams; he brooked no nonsense from anyone and appeared to run the Squadron. We walked out to the Meteor two-seater which the squadron used for instrument flying and I had hardly strapped in before the aircraft was half way out to Waterbeach's runway 23. I remember little of the sortie that was meant to show me the local area as I was half conscious in the back under 90° of bank and what felt like 6G from the time the wheels left the ground until, heaven of heavens, we landed back. Dimly I remembered "Key point this;""....vital to RV here in bad weather";partial consciousness returns again ".........Dog and Duck - once you have found it pull 6G like this and......" (Partial blackout again).

Three days later I was promised a Hunter 6, told that it was heavier than a 4, asked if I had read the notes and then sent out to fly it. Superficially it was like the 4 but with 33% extra power, it promised to be an exciting ride. I strapped in and, when I indicated to the ground crew that I was ready to start, was surprised to see them take cover behind the Auxiliary Power Unit that provided power for starting. I pressed the start button, there was a high pitched 'wheeeee' followed by a huge explosion (well it seemed huge), the cockpit filled with fumes that made my eyes sting and then, from the noise and the smell, there emerged the smooth singing noise of the 200 series Avon. I did not feel very brave as I taxied out and hoped that I would not disgrace my Squadron; I did not but, boy, did the F.6 go well, even though it was carrying an additional 200 gallons under the wings. My second sortie was a high climb and a supersonic dive. I got it sonic, but only just, whereas the F.4s at Chivenor on the last two occasions that I tried, without drop tanks and blast deflectors, had managed 1.1. After my first sortie in the F.6 I asked the ground crew why it was that they had ducked down and hidden behind the APU while I started. They told me that recently there had been several huge explosions caused by the build up of fumes from the Isopropyl Nitrate, a sort of rocket fuel known as AVPIN, that was used to power the starter in lieu of the cartridges in the F.4.

I had arrived on 63 Sqn just as competition for the Fighter Command Weapons Trophy known as the Dacre Trophy, was at its height. Mike Davis was running the squadron effort and had decided that 63 would win it come what may. The Trophy was judged principally on gun sight film tracking a Hunter flying a standard pattern; the No.2 would call 'Commence' to the lead and then had to track the other aircraft as accurately as possible, from 800 yards down to 200, compensating for range and deflection as accurately as possible. Davis was not pleased with my arrival on the Squadron as my efforts had to be part of the Squadron's evaluation total and it was certainly not going to be up to the standard of the others. One day I was down to fly my Dacre weave in the afternoon and Davis came up to me in the coffee bar. "I do not want the Squadron's chances in the Dacre wrecked by you, Haig-Thomas," he said, standing intimidatingly close. "You will be given three films to expose but when you land you will hand in these three films and not the ones with your efforts on." With that he turned and walked away. I put his films in my flying overalls, did as I was told, and 63 won the Dacre Trophy. As a sequel the real boss of the Squadron complimented me on the high ciné scores that I had obtained and no one ever knew the truth.

The Squadron's Meteor had become my obsession. Every time someone flew it, if the back seat was empty, I went in it; I knew the pilot's notes backwards and finally I discovered that the 'A' Flight Commander, Mike Scarrott, was a Meteor instructor. The Meatbox, as it was universally known, had two engines stuck out on the wings and so there was the problem of asymmetric flight to cope with. Mike got me into the front cockpit for the first time and we flew down the great Bedford drains dug by an early Duke of Bedford (well, not personally I suppose) to drain the Cambridge fens. I was told to bring the throttles to idle at 10,000', get the speed down to 125 knots and then open up the port engine to full power, keeping the aircraft straight. The foot load was crushing as the power came on and then the aircraft raised its nose and rolled over on its back. "That's bloody dangerous if you do it trying to land," said the voice from the back and I had to agree with him. We went back to the 'Beach' and flew some circuits and, at the end, an asymmetric one. With Mike's demonstration fresh in my mind, I got the numbers very right. The foot load on the pilot during an asymmetric overshoot was colossal, the rudder bar had to be adjusted so that there was a geometric lock with the leg fully extended and the rudder at maximum deflection, otherwise it just could not be held. The Chief test pilot at Rolls Royce told me many years later that the actual load was 400 lbs so no wonder that any experienced Meteor pilot had raised arches. We flew another dual with lots of asymmetric and then he sent me solo.

The Meteor that I had been flying up to now was the two-seat trainer; its two Derwent engines together produced as much thrust as the Hunter 4 but of course it was devoid of a one ton gun pack. As a consequence it had a very good performance, with speed limited by its thick wing to M.78. My real ambition was the Meteor F.8 in the station flight, the single seat fighter version. One morning I decided to take the bull by the horns and, not due to fly, I took my logbook and walked to Station Flight to ask for a ride in this very good looking camouflaged single-seater. To cut a long story short I was shown the door and walked dejectedly back to 63; as I arrived 'Hooky' Davis was standing outside. "What's the matter Haig-Thomas, you look miserable?" I explained that the Flight Commander running the Station flight would not let me fly his Meteor 8. "Wha'd'yer mean, he wouldn't let you fly?" Mike Davis turned, marched to the Ops desk and picked up the phone. There was a lot of shouting and the phone slammed down. MD came out. "Go and get dressed, there is an F.8 waiting for you." I could hardly believe it. When I arrived back at station flight, the Flight Commander was stammeringly apologetic. "I had not realised that you were the designated tug pilot for air-to-air gunnery, I thought you just wanted to fly a new type and we do not want the RAF to be just a flying club." I apologised for the fact that I had not made it clear earlier. The Meteor F.8 was heaven.

On a routine day flying would typically be a pairs take off in close formation, sometimes just one pair, sometimes two. If there were two pairs the first pulled up into a steep climb and the next pair held themselves low; I was always a second or two behind the leader who would depart at say a 30° angle leaving me slightly below him at 28° and, with a heavy aircraft and that little swept wing, I always felt close to the stall boundary and accepted a very slightly low position on my leader rather than pull myself up level with him. I thought my fears justified when Keith Moore, who had been with me at Chivenor and was flying on 65 Sqn at Duxford, dropped a little low on a pairs take off and pulled the aircraft back up to his leader's level. In doing so the aircraft stalled, rolled, and impacted the ground just off the end of Duxford's 06 runway. Of Keith there was little sign, but in the finest traditions of the service a full size and appropriately weighted coffin was provided for the grieving relatives.

But back to our typical sortie. The two or four aircraft would climb to around 40,000' and split for GCI radar work, taking it in turn to be the bad guys. As fuel ran low we would descend in a tail-chase which tightened and tightened until it became, in effect, a dog fight. Air Combat sounds great and looks great on film but in the days of gun armed jets it was very demanding physically and I found myself fighting to avoid the humiliation of the leader ending up in my six o'clock, or worse still, losing consciousness. I can still remember my G limits in the Hunter; I could pull 7G for 20 seconds, 6G for 60 and 5½ all day. An absolute G limit is quoted for aircraft but for pilots there are two figures, loading and time, which limit a pilot before his vision goes and then the black creeps in until all that can be seen is a dark tunnel as the brain is starved of oxygen. Once this happens, unconsciousness for 20 or 30 seconds follows very quickly and it is essential to relax the G and restore some blood to the brain. Before I started flying I rated myself exceptional fighter pilot material. I was clearly above average at the end of my flying training, average at the end of Chivenor and only too well aware that I was well below average after a month on my first squadron had knocked the over-confidence out of me. I still had a lot to learn.

I had by now acquired nearly as much time in our Meteor and Station Flight's F.8s as I had in the Hunter which never seemed to be serviceable. One day I heard that 25 Sqn were to re-equip with Javelins and would be getting rid of their very graceful long nose NF.14s, a Meteor variant that would never grace my logbook if I did not make an effort to fly it now. As I was not down to fly, armed with my log book to show what an experienced Meteor pilot I was, and my instrument rating card, newly issued, to show that I was Meteor rated, I walked round to 25 Sqn and knocked on the door of the CO. He was busy with the mobile Javelin Conversion Unit but said that if I could find a navigator who would fly with me, I could have an aeroplane. Into 25 Sqn's Crew room I went, expecting to be mobbed by navigators longing to put my legendary name in their logbooks, but to my amazement no one was remotely interested. I was desperate and tried pleading, to no avail, until the door opened and into that room of deadbeats came their youngest navigator/radar operator, one Sergeant Manns, he was bored, loved flying, and rushed to get his flying kit! A flight commander briefed me, authorised the flight and left us together. It was a great day for flying and after starting the engines I tried to motor the hood shut; it shut alright but the dolls eye magnetic indicator remained stubbornly white. I tried the hood three or four times with increasing desperation and then finally I hit the dolls eye, it went black and we were off. The NF.14 was lovely to fly, with a rock like stability that made instrument flying very easy. The great big long nose stretched away in front of me and I had a silly feeling that if I pulled any G it would fall off; I didn't bother with G much as it was no aerobatic aircraft and its good instrument characteristics worked against it in manoeuvring flight. In fact it flew like a heavy aircraft more akin to a Javelin or Canberra than its F.8 or T.7 siblings.

63 Sqn had three flights: 'A' and 'B' were traditional, 'C' flight was the engineering flight and the other two junior pilots and I announced the formation of 'D' flight for 'the younger quieter pilot'. This was the focus of much merriment with the rest of the Squadron, as may be imagined. Mike Seymour was elected 'D' Flight Commander with Trevor Phillips and I as the other members. I mention this only because I am often asked what the fate of all the young pilots on a Squadron was because the average age of a Squadron is always a constant. In Seymour's case he went to Trinity College Cambridge and became a solicitor, and Phillips joined British Airways and became president of the British Air Line Pilots Association. 'C' Flight was our engineering flight, commanded by Warrant Officer Jude, a man who took great pride in his work. One day I was in the coffee bar with several others when the fearsome Warrant Officer entered, walked up to the Squadron CO, saluted and said "Permission to strike an officer please, Sir; it is Pilot Officer Haig-Thomas and he has snagged one of our aircraft when there is nothing wrong with it". "Of course Mr Jude, please carry on," said the boss. Mr Jude came over to me and hit me really hard on the left bicep. That weekend when

I was home and went sailing with my stepfather, who had served as a wartime Major, he asked me what the bruise on my arm was and on being told that I had been hit by the Squadron Warrant Officer muttered "Always were a funny bunch, the RAF".

Mike Seymour and I preferred coffee bars to pubs and in the evening used to enjoy the delights of Cambridge. There were a couple of girls in our favourite coffee bar who seemed to understand the problems of life faced by young fighter pilots especially after they had heard of our incredible bravery and the speed at which we flew. The love of my life was now working in town and my Mother had asked me home one weekend. I had told her that I couldn't come as we were on Summer Exercises and, on Saturday, I set off for London. There is a well known law which encompasses all human activity called Sod's Law (I have no idea who Sod was, but he sure was unlucky) and as the love of my life and I were coming out of Harrods, we came face to face with my mother going in. To her question about how the Summer Exercises were going, I was left tongue-tied; had I been truthful I should have said "'Not according to my hopes – yet".

In September came two pieces of news and in the time-honoured tradition one was good and one was bad. The good news was that we were going to Acklington, north of Newcastle, for some air-to-air gunnery; the bad news was that the Squadron was to be disbanded in October. The engineers worked overtime and all twelve Hunters flew to Acklington. It was my first time in a formation of that size and it felt wonderful. As much the most inexperienced pilot on the Squadron, I flew No.2 to the CO; we ran in up the runway at Acklington and the boss did an incredibly tight break and landing; as No.2 I was next and, quite simply, did not think I could fly a Hunter that tight round finals without leaving a smoking hole half way round the turn and, hopefully a tearful love of my life with a funeral. It is rammed down one's throat during training, "if in doubt go round again." I was in no doubt – I did not believe I could make it so I went round and discovered that this was not the sort of thing the squadron expected on deployments as it did not give a good impression. They were quite right; it does not look good and was most shameful.

After a little while Mike Seymour and I felt a little like those heroes of the great ballad 'Eskimo Nell' so we set out in search of fun. We found it in the little village of Alnwick and, to cut a sordid story short, found ourselves one at each end of a caravan, in a caravan park, with two girls who seemed to understand the pressing requirements of fighter pilots on a gunnery camp. It was dark when our passions were interrupted by the girls' boyfriends who were looking for them. The door was locked but on shining a torch in, one of them saw a leg. Banging on the doors and shaking the caravan left two completely fearless fighter pilots, not to mention the girls, thoroughly alarmed especially when the cuckolds left to get help. Not wishing to cause injuries to a bunch of enraged Geordie miners, Mike and I got dressed and, leaving the girls with memories of the undoubted experiences of their lifetime, made record time to the bus station, just in time to see the last bus leave. With Alnwick not apparently boasting a taxi service, we set out on a very long walk back to base arriving at one in the morning. I scored a big zero on the banner the next day.

We flew back to Waterbeach and the news of the winding up of the Squadron; it was dreadful. 63 had won the Dacre trophy but our F.6 Hunters were to be given to 56 whose Sapphire engined Hunter 5s were to be scrapped. Shortly after we made it home a pair of 56 Hunters were taxiing out past 63 and, as the No.2 appeared to be smoking, the 63 Ops Officer of the day rang 56 to tell them and was reassured that he was not to worry as they always smoked. Not the way we used to see them they didn't and, shortly after take off, - the pilot ejected with an engine failure. I had by now, in addition to flying the Meteor 7, 8 and 14, noticed that the Cambridge UAS had Chipmunks and as there was little to do I asked the boss if I could go over to Marshalls and check out on a piston-engined tail-dragger as I had never flown either. The boss said "Yes" and the Cambridge UAS said "Yes", so over I went, I assumed for a quick circuit dual and then some solo. Oh dear. It took me 3½ hours in four sorties to get to grips with this very different technique and to discover that when it comes to aircraft handling, jets are easy and light tail draggers are also easy but very different. There was much merriment when the news of my progressive failure to solo the Chipmunk was reported back to 63.

A month before we disbanded I was declared 'Operational' and allowed to wear undone the top button of my uniform. This custom originated in WWII and was then the accepted practice for all operational pilots in Fighter Command: it was still the practice in 1958. For me the demise of 63 was a disaster. I was posted to the Hastings Long Range Transport Conversion Unit at Dishforth in Yorkshire and, on my first day there, was told to do up my top button, as that sort of nonsense was not welcome now that I was in Transport Command. It seemed to be symbolic of the end of my life as a single seat pilot.

Chapter 7

DEATH AND REBIRTH

I packed up my trusty little Morris two-seater (built in 1932, she was five years older than me) and set off up the A1 to Yorkshire and Royal Air Force Dishforth to enter a world which was, to me, as dreadful as Waterbeach had been heaven. In those days transport aircraft had two pilots, a flight engineer, a navigator and, quite often a signaller much as they had in WWII - which was not surprising as the aircraft were usually WWII derivatives. I was posted to the Hastings Long Range Conversion Unit together with Derek Christian from 63 Squadron and four others. My crew status was second pilot, a misnomer if ever there was one. The second pilot had to lower and raise the undercarriage and flaps, when told by the Captain, and, when instructed, turn the pitot head heater on and off: absolutely nothing else – no take-offs, no landings, no taxiing - the aircraft was in effect being operated by a single pilot and the passengers were one heartbeat from death. Had the Captain died, and most of them were so old that they looked pretty close to it, I doubt that I could have landed and retained control of the aircraft. The aircraft was very big with four huge Bristol Centaurus sleeve valve engines and it was a tail dragger; if the worst happened I hoped my four hours on chipmunks with Flight Lieutenant Peile at the Cambridge University Air Squadron would prove a help.

It was winter and the Vale of York is not much fun when it is cold and foggy and it is much worse with snow. We had snow. I sat in the right hand seat as various student captains flew circuits and practised their crew management. I knew by heart all the various drills read out by the flight engineer and performed by the geriatric in the left hand seat, but I was allowed to do nothing. One night we landed with lumps of snow everywhere after the runway and taxiways had been bulldozed to enable us to fly. As soon as the aircraft was down and before power had been applied to turn off the runway I raised the flaps to prevent damage from wind-blown ice – Oh dear. The aircraft turned off and his Lordship said "flaps up." "They are up," I replied, proud of my alert airmanship. The heavens opened to a torrent of abuse; under no circumstances was I to touch anything without the captains authority etc etc. For me I am afraid this was my tipping point; I knew what the real world was like and I was not in it. There were two other young Pilot Officers at Dishforth, Tony Weet and Tony Millard, so with myself we were the three Tonys and used to commiserate with each other. Tony Weet was on the Beverley course while Tony Millard was with me on the Hastings and we were not a happy trio. I was unhappiest because I had had a taste of heaven whereas they had gone straight from their flying training to Transport Command - like most of my own flying course.

There were bright spots in my otherwise wretched existence. There were two Chipmunks at Dishforth and Derek Christian and I used to pretend to be Fighter Pilots in endless, ok let me admit, dangerous dog fights, that got quite exciting from time to time. On one occasion after a very long sortie we landed back to find that both our aircraft were, in effect, out of fuel. The Chipmunk's fuel gauges were on the wings, difficult to see, and flight at full power had burnt off much more fuel than either of us thought possible. On another occasion we were flying together in a Chipmunk and had devised a competition against a stopwatch. We each took turns to take off, fly around and land, the time being taken from wheels rolling to wheels stopping. After an hour of this the circuits were getting very dangerous but I suppose Air Traffic found it amusing as very little other flying took place on a normal day. The Wing Commander Flying however did not find our antics at all amusing and ordered us to land, report to him, and explain what we had been doing. He pointed out that our flying was dangerous and stupid and then endeared himself to me enormously by saying that he too had been that sort of pilot once then he gave us a thoroughly deserved weekend as orderly officers, but did it with a smile.

The weather got worse but finally a bright spot appeared in my otherwise gloomy surroundings. Our course was sent to Libya where, in those days, as now, the weather was good in January and February but then, not as now, there was no likelihood of having one's throat cut for upsetting the Prophet Mohammed (peace and blessings etc, etc.) I loved it. The evenings were my first flavour of Arabian life; there was the smell of wood smoke, the barking of pye-dogs and, when it was dark, a sky full of stars and the sound of chirping crickets. It was also the height of the citrus fruit season so I pigged out on tangerines. One day we were sent out to look for a crashed aircraft in the desert; we droned around for several hours and could have flown over it a dozen times and never seen it. I hoped that I would never be waiting for a visual rescue in the desert. We flew home via Malta and I became an enthusiastic tourist but Kodak lost my film taken with the camera given to me as a 21st birthday present by my parents so I lost all my treasured visual mementoes.

On my return home in March, I had to ferry a Chipmunk up to Acklington which was the home of No. 66(F) Squadron. I arrived, checked in and was certainly impressed with the real live rattle-snake kept in their crew room, mercifully in a secure glass case. Their CO, Squadron Leader Peter Bairsto, was very sympathetic to my plight and, like me, couldn't understand why the RAF's top Fighter Pilot was sitting in the right hand seat of a Hastings. He then said that if I could get some time away from Dishforth I could get some proper flying with his Squadron.

I was returned by helicopter to Dishforth and that evening in the mess I saw an advertisement for Fleet Air Arm pilots. The next morning I wrote two letters, one was to their Lordships at the Admiralty asking if they would accept a transfer; and the other was to my CO tendering the resignation of my commission; even my CO agreed I was a square peg in a round hole and agreed to forward it on. I had no wish to leave the RAF, I loved it, but not the sort of RAF that I was in and so I decided, on the grounds that God helps those who help themselves, on one additional line of attack. My old CO of 63 Squadron, 'Sid' Walker, had been posted to the Air Ministry (which must have been as exciting as Transport Command) and his job was to allocate postings for fighter pilots. I took a long weekend in London where the love of my life professed undying and permanent affection - but not quite the way I hoped for and then, on the Monday morning, I went to the Air Ministry and told the doorman that I had come to see Squadron Leader Walker in personnel. I had never seen 'the boss' angry before but he made it quite plain that I was out of order just walking in and demanding an interview; he did not understand my tale of woe and said that resigning my commission was a very serious thing to do and should not be done lightly. He then just said that he could not help me and left.

I returned to Dishforth still on leave, night stopped, and then on to

Acklington to take up the offer of flying with 66 Squadron. They looked after me very well. I flew the Meteor, Vampire and Hunter and remembered what heaven was like, not just for the flying, but for the life and spirit of a Fighter Squadron for a young man in the fifties. On my first Hunter refamiliarisation, I climbed to 30,000 feet and called Finningley for a QGH let-down and a radar approach. I could see Finningley from miles away but the radar could not see me. I had my flaps and wheels down and thought I was at 2,000 feet and then, suddenly, I realised that I had screwed up and I was actually at 12,000 feet. In the fifties cockpits the altimeter was excellent for hundreds and thousands of feet but tens of thousands were determined by a very small third pointer on the dial and most pilots counted the tens subconsciously. A survey, in confidence, had been carried out and almost every pilot admitted that he had got the 10,000 feet level wrong at least once. This came about because of the huge variation in climb performance of various types and marks; I had been counting the tens mentally by Meteor standards and levelled at what I thought was 20,000 feet when I was actually at 30,000 feet. Once the low powered Hunter T.7 two seater came in the same problem worked in reverse; T.7 pilots would think they were at 20,000 feet when they were only at 10,000 and this error, which is obviously much more serious, killed two pilots on 8 Squadron as will be recounted later. 66 Sqn gave me eighteen flights in ten days and I scrounged another four in the Chipmunk. They had no reason to be so generous and it was entirely due to the kindness and sympathy of their boss Squadron Leader Peter Bairsto, a former Officer of the RAF regiment who became a Pilot and ended up as a Knighted Air Marshal.

My time at Acklington over, the little Morris purred southwards down the A1 at 42mph and I arrived back at Dishforth to clear my things up and hear my posting. It was to No.24 Squadron at Colerne in Wiltshire, the only other major UK-based station with Hastings in the transport role although there was a small weather flight in Northern Ireland. My pitifully small worldly possessions were loaded into the trusty Morris which was topped up with fuel, oil and radweld (which seemed to be the only coolant that could be partially retained in the leaky radiator) and I set off for Colerne with a heavy heart. The RAF taught me that 'morale is a state of mind'; I knew what it meant but now that it had proved its point I wished it would back off as my state of mind was bad as it could get.

I arrived back in Colerne on a Monday morning and went to see the adjutant of 24 Squadron. "We don't want you here, you are posted to Aden, flying Venoms and good luck to you." I was stunned. "Why good luck?" I countered. "Very simple, there are fifteen pilots on the Squadron and they have lost six in the last six months. You, dear boy, are on a 24 month tour and unless you are mathematically illiterate you won't need a return ticket." I didn't care; in ten seconds I had gone from death to rebirth. I used the 24 Sqn admin facilities to write to their Lordships withdrawing my naval transfer application, went through the full arrival and departure procedure, a fatuous waste of time that took all day but which was insisted on and then, back in the Morris and home for embarkation leave. I never thanked my old boss Sid Walker for rescuing me but if he ever reads this, which I doubt, thank you Sir.

There was a curious and tragic sequel to my six months and 101 hours as a Transport Pilot which was very sad. Of the three Tonys, I was posted to 8 Squadron which had the worst fatal accident rate in the RAF and am alive, and apparently well, nearly fifty years later. Tony Millard died when his Hastings caught fire in the air and crashed at Khartoum and Tony Weet lies in the upper Yaffa district of South Yemen after his Beverley hit a mountain at night. Flying can be dangerous but with the confidence of youth I knew that I would be all right in my Venom.

Chapter 8

ADEN, NO. 8 SQN AND THE VENOM

All too soon my embarkation leave was over. I caught the train to London and had lunch with the love of my life who then came to Paddington to see me off. I hoped it wasn't in more ways than one but, when the little blue figure waved goodbye as the train pulled out, I suspected that the farewell gesture was both physical and metaphorical which indeed it turned out to be. I have never been of a religious disposition but when, decades later, I heard that she had produced a family I was converted at last to the concept of a virgin birth. The Paddington express, meanwhile, carried me to pastures new. I alighted at Swindon and was taken to a transit camp on a hill which had to be the most dreadfully depressing place ever created. A small collection of wartime huts rejoiced by the name of Royal Air Force Clyffe Pypard; it was cold and damp. I had a filthy supper and went to bed. Tomorrow, I was to fly to Aden on a Comet C.2 from Royal Air Force Lyneham and left England on a cold grey May 5th 1959. Even in those days, politics being what they are, the RAF could not fly direct to Aden so our route was Lyneham – Malta – Kano, in Nigeria, for a night stop and then on to Aden via Nairobi the next day. The Comet impressed me; 'people' simply did not travel by jet in the fifties. We landed at Malta, refuelled, and then on to Kano. This was the first time I had smelled Africa, a hot dry distinctive scent which has to come from the reddish African soil. As I walked over the tarmac to the airport buildings a row of vultures were perched along the top of the airport roof eyeing the newcomers; I hoped we did not crash on take off.

There were only four officers on the aeroplane, the most senior being a Group Captain and the rest of us junior in varying degrees right down to a Pilot Officer, myself, still in this lowly rank as my full worth had yet to be recognised by her Majesty. At dinner the Group Captain had been in full flow but eventually I felt brave enough to ask him about his tie. 'That tie is a Squadron tie' he replied, 'Which Squadron?' I countered without realising that I had fallen into an elephant trap, 'It is not 'a' Squadron it is 'the' Royal Yacht Squadron'. I did not realise quite how smart the Royal Yacht

Squadron was until many years later but, feeling uncomfortable, I left the little party after supper and watched a Rhodesian Air Force DC-3 land, taxi in and shut down. The crew got out and the co-pilot turned out to be Ollie Sutton who I had known well at both Ludgrove and Eton. I had another dinner with him and then a late night reminiscing. The following morning we photographed each other outside the Comet before my departure and said goodbye; the next time we met and had dinner together was in Geneva thirty years later where he was editor of Air International.

The flight to Aden via Nairobi was uneventful and we arrived after dark on May 6th; I was one of the last off the plane and as I stepped out of the Comet a blast of heat hit me, from the jet pipes I thought until, with a shock, I realised that this was Aden in the hot season. I wanted to turn round and go home thinking it was not possible to survive in temperatures and humidity levels that high. I have referred to Aden because that was the name of the town which formed the colony and was built in and around two extinct volcanoes with little Aden ten miles West of Aden proper. Little Aden was home to the Shell oil refinery and, during my time there, a squadron of armoured cars from the Life Guards who were succeeded by a similar detachment from the 11th Hussars as they were then known. The hinterland of the colony was a UK protectorate split into two and known rather unoriginally, but very practically, as the West Aden protectorate (WAP) and the East Aden protectorate (EAP). The protectorates stretched for six hundred miles along Southern Arabia with the WAP bordering on the Yemen and the EAP Saudi Arabia to the North and Oman to the East. The WAP border was well understood by both parties but in those days Saudi Arabia claimed that their border stretched all the way to the sea, a recipe for certain conflict which, miraculously, was avoided when eventually the two protectorates and Aden colony merged with the Yemen to become Yemen. Just to the North of Aden town was Khormaksar, a giant air force base with 37 Squadron flying Shackletons, a four-engined derivative of the Lancaster, and 30 Squadron with Blackburn Beverleys, a huge square box with wings on top and four Bristol Centaurus engines. The Beverleys flew at 145 knots and were used to supply the army 'up country' at the four sand strips that could take them. Also used for army support was 78 Squadron with Scottish Aviation Twin Pioneers, a very slow flying twin engined aircraft with a fixed undercarriage and two 550 hip Alvis

Leonides engines. There was also a Canberra and a Hastings for use by the Commander-In-Chief, and two Percival Pembrokes for dropping off personnel up country, duplicating the role of the 'Twin Pins' but for people not freight. Last but not least was 8 Squadron with 18 Venoms and two Vampire T11s; 8 Squadron shared a hangar with the Arabian Peninsular Reconnaissance Flight who were equipped with four Meteor FR9s and a T.7. This was my new home.

On the morning of May 7th I awoke early, breakfasted and hastened on foot and in the heat to 8 Squadron. There I met Andy Devine, my Flight Commander who had flown F-86 Sabres in Korea with the USAF and he took me up to see my boss, Squadron Leader Rex Knight, also a Korean War Sabre Pilot. The Squadron adjutant Barry Wylam brought some papers into the office and, being a curious type, when he and the boss went out for a moment, I had a look at some other papers on the boss's desk. The signal on top of the pile was to inform the Squadron of my posting; on it the boss had written 'who is this chap, do we want him?' Probably not was the answer, but dear me, I certainly needed them. My interview over, it was down to the crew room to see if I could get someone to put me on the flying programme. 'No' was the answer, so I went next door to the Meteor Flight to let them know that another Meteor qualified, current, and instrument-rated pilot of exceptional ability had arrived. Their T.7 was serviceable, and not being flown, so Sam Small was authorised to show me the operational area. Soon we were airborne and heading North at low level down the winding road through the mountains that led to Dhala, an army camp on the Yemen border beyond which were the baddies trying to destabilise loyal tribes in the Aden protectorate on behalf of their communist paymasters. I found the low level operational flying very exciting. Soon Sam pulled up and flew over some mountains further east to show me Al Qara, a pretty medieval town built on a pinnacle of rock. I had no idea that, later on, however pretty it might have been I would have to knock down one of the houses. We flew round it twice and then suddenly Sammie Small said 'Look at that bastard shooting at us from the roof of that house'. In the back seat, and under a sudden and violent increase in 'G' loading, I was not sure that to do an aggressive low pass was a particularly good idea with someone actively shooting at us. Perhaps the baddie would run out of ammo before we got too close.

Two days later, and after another Meteor recce, Andy Devine put me down for an acceptance check in the Vampire T.11 and then, he said, I could fly the Venom. I flew the Vampire, passed a quiz on the Venom and was scheduled for a solo the next morning. The Venom was a pilot's dream. On my first solo I was the only one flying from the Squadron as the other aircraft were being prepared for 'ops' the next day. I completed my general handling including a compressibility run up to the M.88 limit, where it was just as twitchy as the little Vampire F.5 on which I had trained, and then returned to the Khormaksar overhead for a practice flameout landing. The sky was blue and the visibility unlimited, unusual for that time of year, as I set up my flame out pattern at 12,000ft. Suddenly I heard a pair of Venoms call for taxi, they were being flown by two ferry pilots from England to 208 Squadron, our sister unit in Nairobi. The pair got airborne and then, suddenly, I heard 'Red Leader turning down wind for immediate landing' 'Roger Lead do you have a problem?' replied the tower. 'Negative my ammo. door has come open. I will land and have it closed.' They were the last words he spoke; the aircraft flicked and spun in from around 600ft; a huge pillar of black smoke rose up to me. I flew round it a couple of times at 10,000ft and then, remembering that 8 Squadron had lost seven Venoms and six pilots in the previous six months, decided to do a nice wide, gentle circuit before landing. That was not quite the end of the story as Andy Devine came out of our crew room and, not aware that there were any Venoms in transit, saw one turning crosswind after take off then crash and burn. He knew that I was the only aircraft airborne so he ran up to the boss's office to tell him that the new pilot had crashed and was definitely dead. The boss rang the Wing Commander flying who told the Group Captain, at which point I taxied into the Squadron's apron to everyone's relief - mine too. Perversely one of the recent run of 8 Squadron 'fatals' had been caused by the same problem with the ammunition door. These two small panels just behind the cockpit covered the ammunition tanks and were the only place for a pilot to put any belongings or clothes. I do not think, even today, that anyone knows whether the pilot stalled in the turn at nearly maximum all up weight, or if the open door caused a breakdown of the airflow over the tail plane. If I had to guess, it would be the former as both Vampire and Venom, although fitted with wings of different sections, were very prone to violent departures at low speed.

One of the wonderful things about flying in Aden was the weapons range five miles from the airfield, and every Thursday and Friday we were 'on the range'. The object of a fighter aircraft is to deliver weapons, accurately, and this can only be done by constant practice; there is, and has to be, a presumption that flying an aircraft comes instinctively and naturally to any Squadron pilot but accurate weapons delivery simply does not; it is an acquired art that requires constant practice. The next day Andy Devine decreed that I was to accompany the Range Safety Officer to see how it was done. We drove out in a Squadron Land Rover across the sun-baked gypsum to the range. A mile from the RSO's safety hut a human skeleton lay on its back, its bones bleached very white in the baking tropical sun. No one seemed to think that the skeleton was unusual or worthy of comment. It was just that life in a third world country, albeit a British colony was different from the Home Counties. On the range there were four air-to-ground gunnery targets, large metal frames covered with Hessian. Pilots fired ball, non-explosive, ammunition at them after which the holes in the target were counted and marked with black so as to avoid double scoring. There was something magic about the noise made by a fighter firing its cannon; I had never heard it before and couldn't wait to go 'live' and do it myself. After each gun attack, as the aircraft cleared the range, twenty or thirty Arabs would rush to collect the solid brass 20mm cannon shell casings. Presumably it was one of these that I had seen in skeletal form on my way out who on his unlucky day had only collected one shell casing. There were two huts on the range, one for the RSO and the other for the range ground staff; from these huts bearings were taken of the impact of our three inch unguided second world war rockets as they struck the ground somewhere near, but seldom on, an old lorry that was the RP (Rocket Projectile) target.

My conversion flying went well and at the end of May I had flown fourteen hours, eight scrounged on Meteors, five on Venoms and one in the Vampire: another thank-you prayer for my Meteor conversion. Andy said it was time I went on the range. The trusty old Vampire was loaded with three-inch rockets and one gun with fifty rounds of 20 mm 'ball'. For air to ground precision firing we used the fixed cross placing it on the target and firing a short sighter burst; if the rounds were blown ten metres to the right of the target one merely placed the fixed cross a similar distance to the left on the next pass and, hey presto, the rounds shredded the Hessian – in theory. With my youthful lack of intelligence and common sense it had never occurred to me that wind could blow a bullet at all but I could see that it obviously did. Rocketry was more difficult. It was necessary to track the target for four seconds using the gyro gunsight and then press the RP firing button on the stick. The rockets then fired with a swooshing noise and the immediate application of around five and a half G was necessary to prevent the aircraft from hitting the ground. Andy gave me a brief during which I was told to roll onto the target, uncage the gunsight, wait until I was terrified, count four slowly, then fire the rocket, and pull like hell. "If you see your rocket hit the ground then you are dead," he added. We went on the range, fired all four rockets, fired out the gun, and landed back in thirty minutes. I was very tired but oh boy was it fun!

As luck would have it, with weapons work I appeared to have found something for which I did actually have some ability for. I loved going on the range and Thursday and Friday were my favourite days; there was intense competition each day for the top-scoring pilot at both air-to-ground gunnery and RP. The RP's were not always very accurate – sometimes on pressing the button nothing would happen, the pilot would then call "hang up." On other occasions after pressing the button, nothing would happen and then a second or two later the rocket would fire; the pilot would then call "slow burner." At other times the fins on the RP would be misaligned, and on firing the RP from under the wing it would appear in front of the windscreen with a small intense flame until the application of the high G recovery and the effect of gravity on the missile caused it to disappear; for this the pilot would call "twirler". With any of these the score was not counted. It took me some time to master the technique of firing the rockets and then one day I did it. To win the day's RP shoot it was necessary to have not more than one "hang up", "slow burner" or "twirler" out of the four missiles; two made the shoot non-effective and here lies one of the great tragedies of my life which, absurdly, rankles to this day as some small things do. I was cleared in live by the RSO for a four rocket precision attack. I fired the first one. There was the usual delay as the observers agreed the fall, then "direct hit". I was elated. The same thing happened with my second and third RPs so my average error was an unheard of zero and I had a valid three weapon shoot. I should then have cheated, turned in, tracked the target and, not firing, called "hang up" – I didn't and my fourth RP impacted seventeen yards at 12 o'clock; I won the day with an average of four and a quarter yards but it could have been zero. How stupid could I get? Unknown to me our Station Commander, Group Captain John Merrifield DSO DFC AFC who, during WWII, had found the German Peenemunde rocket site in a PR Mosquito, was on the range with the RSO and had observed my three direct hits; he then made some very kind comments on my weapons when he came down to 8 Squadron the next day. Then it was his turn to impress me. He had not flown a Venom for several months but booked a ride on the range and came top in air-to-ground gunnery and third with the RPs. He was always very kind and supportive of me, especially when I was in trouble later on in my tour; tragically he was killed in a helicopter accident out of Upavon shortly after returning home.

Being very young and keen - I was just twenty-one - and not yet having succumbed to the effects of heat, I used to volunteer for air tests which were usually done in the afternoons when the engineers had completed their work. One day, after an engine change, Andy let me do the air test. It was very hot and very humid throughout the hot season from May 1st to September 30th (normally 95 degrees with 95% humidity). I signed off the paper work, had a brief from the Chief Tech and got airborne. Engine tests require the recording of RPM, Jet Pipe Temperature and time every 5000ft from brakes off to 40,000ft. Everything went well and I topped out at what in those days we called 'Angels 40', so much better than the contemporary and absurd, 'Flight Level Four Zero Zero'. I then noticed a line of massive thunderclouds formed when the hot humid air from the Red Sea is forced upwards by the Hijaz Mountain Range which runs down the SW Arabian littoral; I wondered how high the clouds were. The Venom was still climbing and soon I found that I was being squeezed into a tiny flight envelope limited by the Venom's clean stall of 105 knots at 1G, and the Mach meter which was close to its limit of M.88 with only 135 knots indicated on my ASI. In effect, I had 30 knots between the low speed and the mach stall. Not at all healthy. My altimeter read 57,000ft which the met office later corrected to give me 58,500ft. My little Venom was still climbing as it got lighter and lighter and would certainly have made the magic 60,000ft, but only because I was in the tropics where the temperatures at very high altitudes are much colder than in the UK; most amazingly the tops of the big thunder clouds were at least another 10,000ft above me. I eventually flew 100 Venom sorties and, on two occasions, an enormous explosion in the cockpit was caused by a ruptured hood seal; had the hood seal blown when I was at altitude, and when it was mostly likely to do so, I would have been dead in seconds as the blood boiled off in my lungs. Once again I had been incredibly stupid. Back at base I had trouble; there was a notice in the crew room saying 'HT, you are to see the adjutant at once'. I walked to Station Headquarters in the heat having had a lift down in the morning after leaving my newly acquired Fiat 500 at the mess. The adjutant kept me waiting; I had no idea anyone worked in the afternoons as the standard working hours were 0700 to 1300. Eventually my turn came. "Ah Haig-Thomas – The Group Captain wishes you to remove your car from the officers mess bar immediately". While I had been flying, my car had been manoeuvred into the bar and now monopolised half of the room. I was not very pleased and had to recruit several Arabs to help get it out; it took ages. It was nothing to do with the Station Commander; all the time the adjutant had been in on the joke perpetrated by my squadron colleagues.

Life was not entirely about flying. I was recruited for the squadron cricket team and played polo, both very badly. One day the brigadier who ran the polo ponies asked me to take over as officer i/c. but I sensibly declined and then, after missing an easy catch and scoring a duck, I got dropped from the squadron cricket team. From then on I flew air tests, went to the beach or had a nap in the afternoons and played bridge in the evenings. At least two thirds of the pilots on 8 Squadron were Rhodesian or South African nationals on their second or third fighter tours; they had a wonderful relaxed style of life and were great sportsmen and natural pilots. One day, shortly after I had joined the Squadron, Barry Raffle arrived an hour late for work having been up all night attending to a nurse. He went to the end of the crew room and went to sleep. Andy Devine was in despair over the lack of discipline in his pilots as Barry was still asleep when he should have been on the range; he woke him and sent him out to fly. An hour later he was again fast asleep on the sofa having won the day's top score with both guns and RP; I was impressed. The next day I was even more impressed when Andy, determined to make his unruly flight more professional, had an oral quiz on the aircraft speeds and limitations, large numbers of which need to be known to fly any jet. Barry got several wrong including the undercarriage lowering speed; even I thought my hero a little amateurish but if the amateur came top on the range he obviously had something to offer the Air Force.

Aden was a key coaling station in the nineteenth century on the route out to India, Singapore and the Antipodes and its life had been modelled on life in India whence it was governed. In 1959 it had its own governor who acted for the Queen via the colonial office. The working hours were 7am to 1pm, very agreeable, leaving the afternoons free for a life at the Tarshyne Officers' Club which had a lovely beach and a bar. The beach was protected by a shark net strung across the bay after a Wing Commander's wife died from shock and blood loss following a shark attack while only wading waist deep. I had a pair of fins and a mask and one day decided to swim along the net, on the safe side, duck diving to around ten feet and then surfacing for air every fifteen yards or so. When I arrived in the middle of the bay it was very rough, as always in the hot season. I took a deep breath and dived down again to find to my horror a hole in the shark net big enough to accommodate a nuclear submarine, let alone a shark. A biblical re-enactment occurred as I ran to the beach on top of the water. All in all life was heaven; I loved the flying and the beach life but hated the heat and the lack of female company of which I was reminded by letters of diminishing intensity from the love of my life back home.

The heat was very bad news in the Venom; the cold air unit was designed for UK latitudes and medical trials recorded cockpit temperatures of 170 degrees F on the cockpit floor, under the ejection seat. Trials were done one day; six pilots put on their overalls and Mae Wests and then each walked to a Venom climbed in and shut the hood for ten minutes and then climbed out to simulate a low level flight. A total time of twenty minutes from weigh-in to weigh-in produced a minimum weight loss of five pounds and a maximum of just over seven; it mattered little since as soon as anyone landed they would go to the fridge in the crew room and drink at least one, and occasionally two, bottles of water or squash to replace the fluid loss. Our overalls were disgusting. Six pounds of sweat once or twice a day and never washed! The Air Force issue was one pair of overalls per person and the 24-hour dhobi service meant that if you had them washed you could not fly the next day as they were away at the laundry. Under no circumstances did anyone wish to borrow anyone elses! Although conditions for pilots were on the limits of endurability the conditions for the ground crew were much worse; the armourers in particular had to lie on their backs on the sandy gypsum to replace the gun doors. Their bodies were soaked in sweat, and the gypsum stuck to their backs; yet their morale was surprisingly good with even less grumbling than when in the UK. We just all knew how awful it was and that we had to live with it. Neither the ground crew nor pilots had any air-conditioning, just the ubiquitous fans turning slowly in every ceiling. Years later, after the UK Government had left Aden, the Russians took it over to further their ambitions in Arabia. I used to enjoy the thought of the sweat and those slowly turning fans, being enjoyed by Ivan and his comrades.

Occasionally I would wonder at the things we did. Weapons, for example, were obviously very dangerous and they were all fired electrically. To be safe pilots climbed in, started up and then flying on the range or operationally we taxied forward, came to a halt, and then hung our arms out of the cockpit while the master armament plug was inserted. All guns and rockets were now live and could be fired by the trigger or RP button on the control column. One day I taxied out, hung out my arms and, once the plug was in, taxiied forward and turned right onto Khormaksar's long taxiway. A hundred yards in front of me was a BOAC Britannia with a full load of happy passengers all oblivious to the fact that a hundred yards behind it sat Pilot Officer Haig-Thomas with four live 3inchRPs andfour live 20mm cannonwithmyhands and fingers inevitably all over and on the firing buttons. I was very careful. On another day a BOAC Britannia provided a delightful piece of humour. The BOAC Britannia touched down, bounced high into the air and then crunched down on the 09 runway. John Dowling was quick to the phone "Compliments of No.8 Squadron to the Captain of the Britannia on the worst landing any of us has seen by any airliner anywhere" - Half an hour later back came the reply thanking us for our compliments and saying that it was the worst landing he too had ever seen, or experienced, but that he had a new co-pilot, just joined from the RAF, that he was trying to train. Game love.

8 Squadron was large by Fighter Squadron standards and the pilots had duties other than just flying. For example we provided the adjutant at

RAF Salalah, a route station in Oman 600 miles along the South Arabian coast line from Aden and, in addition, had to send pilots 'up country' with the army convoys in case they were ambushed. My first trip was to Dahla seventy miles North of Aden; it was very dusty and took all day each way. I put my goggles on my hat and had a photograph taken looking, I thought, for all the world like Rommel in the North African desert. There was no shooting for which I was thankful - but a near miss with a Scorpion in my tent made me realise how wise I had been to join the RAF and not the army. Sometimes we were flown to an army camp for a week in case it was shot up; on one of these occasions it was a detachment commanded by Lt Col Bernard Briggs. BB loved 8 Squadron but he loved beat-ups even more. When he had a pair of Venoms to work he would command a beat up, the quality of which was judged by the quantity of sand blown into his beer as he stood outside the mess tent, mug in hand. He was very proud of his profile and appearance and always wore a triangular piece of the Times (it had to be the Times, no other paper was of sufficient quality) taped to his nose to prevent sunburn as, he informed me, women disliked sunburnt noses. Rumours of his attractiveness to errant wives abounded, so perhaps I should have tried the same as my love life had come to a total halt in Aden where girls were as rare as the proverbial rocking-horse excrement. Once, at a camp surrounded by hills, as dusk fell the army fired-in their machine guns onto fixed points. The soft glowing red tracer rounds floated across the valleys like red tennis balls, occasionally hitting a rock, and ricocheting off at 90 degrees. I loved it. The Colonel told me that when he returned to England he wanted to command the military prison at Shepton Mallett and would give cocktail parties at which half the guests would be murderers or rapists. The non-custodial guests would have to guess whether they were talking to a murderer, rapist or just another guest. With hindsight I think the Colonel must have spent too much time in Arabia, but his parties sounded fun.

Naturally enough, as a young fighter pilot I was completely fearless, or nearly so, because like the Gilbertian Admiral who was hardly ever sick at sea my lack of fear did not extend to snakes, scorpions or giant fast running spiders. On one trip I faced all three. There had been trouble in the Wadi Sayeed, a quiet, peaceful and green valley, marred only by a tendency for its residents to shoot at people. The boss sent me off and, having been dropped at Ataq by Pembroke, I drove south in a Land Rover and found a mud fort together with an officer of the 11ᵗʰ Hussars, Michael Moore; it was late afternoon and Michael said that we were joining the local Sheikh for our evening meal. We walked to the Sheikhs house, took off our shoes and sat round a huge feast of goat, which is not one of my favourite foods.Any piece of meat I chose always seemed to have raw looking pipes sticking out of it; the Sheikh finally did for me by selecting a piece of wind pipe with a bit of the lungs still attached, and then chewed off what I knew from my biology lessons were cartilaginous rings. I had only just started trying to learn Arabic and the conversation was completely lost on me; however Michael Moore said that they had told him there were some bad men in the hills. The next morning he and I were to walk down the valley and, when they shot at us, I would call in a Venom strike to kill them. I wasn't over keen on the battle plan as I didn't fancy being shot at but I might win a VC so I went to sleep on it even more convinced than ever that I was right to join the Air Force, suicide not being my thing.

Each day a pair of my lucky mates in Venoms arrived; Michael told me where the baddies were and I ordered a full war load of 20mm HE shells to kill them. Michael liked the sound of fighter cannon as much as I did; the pilots loved it and no one got killed. I thought it most satisfactory. The most memorable feature of life in up-country Arabia was the silence, an occasional cock crow and the smell of wood smoke. I could quite understand how some men were completely captivated by it and were happy to live a very lonely life by themselves; but then they did not have the range on Thursdays and Fridays to look forward to as I did. These men lived alongside, and with, the Arab communities and sent their reports to the Aden Intelligence Service. They had usually been through the Foreign Office-run Middle East Centre for Arabic Studies in Beirut, (a school for spies if ever there was one,) and so spoke fluent Arabic.

On my third day at Sayeed I went down to the bottom of our Mud fort. In one room the cook was kneeling on the floor kneading the dough to make bread for Michael and I and the four Arabs from the Aden Protectorate Levies who were our guards. As the cook kneaded the dough great drops of sweat fell from his brow and were kneaded in for added flavour with, presumably, a little of that essential Middle east requirement, salt. I passed the cook and went into the little room with a bucket to commune with nature; shutting the badly fitting door, something caught my eye. There by the top hinge held in the crack by its head and thrashing with great vigour, was a snake. I had a problem. I was wearing an Arab loincloth with no shoes or shirt and, if I opened the door, the snake would fall to the floor I would be bitten and then suffer an agonising and slow death. I had no idea what sort of snake it was but I knew it was deadly because it was a snake and I could just tell. Feeling a little pathetic I shouted 'Hanash, Hanash, Fi Hanash Hinna' and in no time there were lots of non-English speaking Arabs jabbering outside who eventually fetched Michael Moore. The final plan was for me to open the door and take a flying leap out of the loo where an Arab with a stick would then dispatch the snake. I opened the door and jumped, the snake fell to the ground and disappeared into a hole in the wall behind the bucket. If anyone reading this should find himself in the Wadi Sayeed he should be careful how he treads round the far side of a big rock near the old APL fort as I never used the bucket indoors again.

After the snake excitement, walking the Wadi to entice people to give themselves away by shooting at us was positively boring; my Squadron colleagues each fired out another 800 rounds of 20 mil; Michael told me they were right on target. I told the pilots and we adjourned to the fort. It was very hot and to avoid snakes (not that they worried me) I elected to sleep on top of our fort under an open-sided sun shelter. At around midnight I was awakened by one of our guards killing a scorpion a few yards from my bed but then I went to sleep again until I was reawakened by something falling on my chest; shining my torch on the roof of the shelter I saw an enormous Camel Spider staggering across the roof, upside down, dislodging pieces of mud as it did so. This was the end; Michael Moore thought it amusing but I watched the sky lighten and a new day dawn without attempting any further sleep. Michael thought all the baddies had been killed so I took my Land Rover and driver back to Ataq; a Pembroke flew me home.

Chapter 9

METEOR TALES

The Arabian Peninsular Reconnaissance Flight (APRF) had four pilots and four Meteor FR.9s for low level fighter reconnaissance work with a two seat Meteor T.7 for training, communications andinstrument flying. The previous summer, on 63 Squadron, I had renewed my Vampire instrument rating on the Meteor as soon as I had checked out on the type. A Meteor rating was valid for any multi-engine aircraft but the Vampire only for single engine types so in Aden, although flying Venoms and Hunters operationally, I flew my annual instrument check in the Meteor which otherwise I could not have flown. I was a secret admirer of the four Fighter Recce pilots not because they were all hugely experienced, being second or third tourists, but because they had all flown Swifts in Germany, a type which had hooked itself into my psyche at Valley when, as I have recounted earlier, the F.7 had lit its afterburner at low level over my head.

Shortly after I arrived the T.7 was being flown to Mogadishu in East Africa by a Flt Lt Bradshaw. A flight this long was possible if flown high level with full mains, ventral and pylon tanks however when he arrived in the general vicinity of Mogadishu he was desperately short of fuel and had suffered total electric failure above solid cloud. Unable to let down blind he jumped out and, descending by parachute, landed neatly on the beach whence he was rapidly rescued. A few hundred yards to his left and the sharks of the Indian ocean would have had him while if a mile or so to the right he would have been big cat food; one had to admire the precision of his blind parachute descent through cloud. Clearly experience had paid dividends to allow him such an exact landing between these two perils.

A new Meteor was rapidly delivered from England, there being plenty of this obsolete type available and, not long after, one of the other APRF pilots, 'Porky' Munro, flew it down to Nairobi. Unfortunately he ran short of fuel before he got there and, to everyone's amazement, he landed it wheels down in the African bush expecting to wipe off the undercarriage and slide to a halt in the remains. Instead he rolled to a halt in six-foot high elephant grass with the aircraft undamaged; presumably he was saved from becoming cat food by being able to hide in the Meteor at night when the purring noises grew too loud. Even more amazingly, after he was found, the elephant grass was cleared; a Beverley flew in with fuel in drums and the Meteor was then flown out, landing safely in Nairobi.

One day there were no Venoms to fly so I went next door to see if I could scrounge a Meteor, only to find a heated argument taking place between Tai Retief, the APRF Flight Commander, and Porky. In a nutshell, Tai said that you could not take a blurred photograph of a Land Rover using $1/2000^{th}$ of a second shutter speed; Porky said you could. Two days later I saw a picture of a Land Rover that looked like a stretched version of a New York stretch Limo with the aperture and exposure time confirmed on the bottom of the photograph, I was amazed. 'Porky' said that he had been ten feet out and ten feet up at 400 knots which must have been exciting for the occupants of the Land Rover if they had not seen him coming. 'Porky' became a good friend and I discovered that during his flying training he had bailed out after a mid-air collision with another student doing unauthorised formation aerobatics and, on another occasion, landed wheels up in a field after running out of fuel. Life in the RAF in the fifties was clearly more relaxed than later on as he got his wings on time with only a few extra orderly officers' duties to compensate Her Majesty for the wrecked aircraft. 'Porky' or Tony as I am reminded by his wife that he is to be called nearly fifty years later, became CO of the Sultan of Muscat and Oman's Air Force and then suffered a debilitating stroke soon after his retirement.

Manx Kelly was the third of the four pilots and he and I flew together a lot as a pair when the APRF joined up with 8 Squadron. Manx was a true eccentric, an exceptional handling pilot and brilliant artist. One day I was preparing for my instrument rating in the back seat with Manx in the front as safety pilot; we were flying with one engine flamed out and me 'under the hood'. Suddenly Manx said "I have it, I have just spotted Porky in an FR.9 and he hasn't seen us". He pulled the Meteor vertically upwards, executed a perfectly flown stall turn, relit the starboard engine on the way down and turned in for a high quarter attack. As we closed to four hundred yards he mimicked a machine gun with a 'Tukka Tukka Tukka' on the radio – nothing else was said but it provoked an instantaneous 'break' towards us followed by a memorable (when I was conscious) one v. one dog fight. Manx announced that my instrument flying was fine so we went low flying instead. He was the founder in the mid sixties of the Rothmans aerobatic team, and was tragically killed flying an experimental home built aeroplane in American when it developed 'flutter'. It disintegrated, leaving Judy and four children without husband and father.

One day we were briefed that some heavy machine guns had arrived at Al Qara and we were not to fly near the place. Unfortunately, Al Qara was a very picturesque town on top of a pinnacle of rock in the upper Yaffa district North East of Aden and Manx had just acquired a new Japanese cine camera. He thought Al Qara would make a nice shot for the film he was making of flying in Aden. He throttled back, dropped one third flap and flew slowly past the town cine camera in hand; his filming was rudely interrupted however and on landing it was found that he had thirty-eight bullet holes in his aircraft. The squadron engineering officer said that the aircraft was to be written off but the Group Captain overruled him as it was his favourite Meteor and, in spite of the four hundred man hours required to repair it, repair it they must. Eventually, three months later it, was done and Manx took off for an air test which, naturally, included a lot of low flying, that is until he collided with an Egyptian Vulture, which finally did for the aircraft what the thirty eight bullets had failed to do and the aircraft was scrapped.

This however was not the end of Manx's excitements. At the beginning of 1961 Ken Hayr arrived on 8 Squadron and, there being no Hunters serviceable, Manx offered to show him around the area. Naturally the beauty of Al Qara was on the menu but, while they were flying over it, a distinct thud announced that they had been hit and, on landing back at Khormaksar, a bullet was found lodged in the parachute under Ken Hayr's seat. The next day Manx promised Ken a less exciting sortie to the north east to show him the army camp at Ataq and the Wadi Sayeed to the south of it. Manx ordered the fuel tanks, including the pylon tanks under the wings, to be filled and they took off. They were nearing the end of the low level part of the exercise when Ken heard Manx exclaim "Oh my God". The aircraft's nose pitched up and both engines went to full power; on enquiring the nature of the problem Ken was told that they were down to a 40/40 fuel state (80 gallons) which was the normal landing fuel. At 30,000ft both engines flamed out and the aircraft entered a glide, with appropriate distress calls to base.Almost unbelievably they crossed the runway threshold from a straight in approach rolling to a halt half way down the asphalt. The usual array of ambulances, fire trucks, engineering officers and the curious surrounded the aeroplane, led by the Squadron SNCO in charge of the flight line. Manx, furious, climbed out – "I told you to fill the pylon tanks chief you bloody nearly killed us". "I did so sir" and, patting the pylon tanks, "They are still full sir you must have forgotten to select them". They were and he had! In the FR.9 that the APRF normally flew, the pylon and ventral tanks fed automatically but in the T.7 they had to be selected manually which Manx had forgotten to do and they had then 'dead sticked' the jet with 200 gallons of unused fuel still on board. After these excitements Ken stuck to the Hunters. I had first met him on 66 Squadron at Acklington, and I met him again when he was a Flight Commander on 19 Squadron at Leconfield. Many years later, in 2000 in fact, after he had retired as Air Marshal Sir Kenneth but was still actively flying, I strapped him into a Vampire at the Biggin Hill Air Show and then watched him spin in ten minutes later when he encountered the tip vortices of a Sea Vixen. The aircraft rotated fast three times and then exploded, producing that, by now all too familiar great black mushroom cloud. With him when he died was another Vampire pilot, Jim Kerr, who I had just checked out in his own aircraft. A sad day.

The fourth pilot in the APRF was Fred Trowern or 'Fat Fred' as he was irreverently known. Fred was a father of five and never did anything wrong. Operationally he was exceptional and on one occasion in an area that had become politically very hot, he flew low level down a valley and noticed a rope in the mouth of a cave that had not been there two days earlier. As a true professional he did not go back for another look but briefed a pair of strike Hunters who each salvoed four rockets with HE into the cave mouth, killing a small group of baddies hiding out from the ground forces who were looking for them.Fred Trowern is still flying at Middle Wallop, aged 65, teaching Army Air Corps pilots their basic fixed-wing flying before they graduated to helicopters and was one of the surprisingly few 8 Squadron pilots to survive to old age.

By the time I had left the Middle East I had flown a total of 113 Meteor sorties totalling just over 100 hours and never had a frightening moment or technical malfunction of any sort during that time. A wonderful aircraft.

Chapter 10

MORE VENOM IN ADEN

I strapped on my revolver, popped a bag of .45 ammo in a pocket of my flying overalls, slipped on a Mae West lifejacket and met up with Al Withington who was to fly with me as my No.2 that day. Four months had passed since I arrived in Aden and my resurrection from the grave of Transport Command was now a long past, half remembered, nightmare. I had been briefed to lead a pair on a 'flag wave' over a small village at the top of the Mukerias escarpment which had been the subject of friendly approaches by the baddies in the Yemen; the politicos had decided to remind them of the awesome power of Her Majesty's long arm - which was me. I thought she had made an excellent choice. The flying was simple, and the navigation easy, which was probably why I had been given it as one of my first 'leads'. As we flew low level over the Laudar Plain I saw, as if in slow motion, an Arab walking along a mile ahead with his back to us; he stopped, turned round and, taking his rifle off his shoulders, took aim and fired. I knew he had fired because I could very clearly see the puff of smoke from his rifle, probably an old Martini Henry of First World War vintage. I was very close by the time he fired as, at a mile every seven seconds, it does not take long to overtake an Arab on foot a mile ahead. Turning hard away from him, and with Al following, I pulled up into a great arcing wingover to the right through 270° and came back at him low level with no evil intent but just to show him that we had noticed and to give him a fly-by. When I was at around two hundred yards he suddenly threw himself flat on the ground as he probably thought he was going to be shot, something that had not even crossed my mind, although he may have sensed that he was staring at Wyatt Earp behind four 20 mm cannon, so perhaps his reaction was understandable. Al and I turned back through 90° and continued on our way to our authorised flag wave leaving our, by now dusty, Arab to continue his journey. I write of this trivial incident only because I was amazed how, in four months, I had changed from the horror of actually being shot at in the Meteor with Sam Small, and his predilection for beating up the miscreant, to doing the same thing myself.

There were many variations to our day-to-day operational flying. We used methodology transposed direct from the N.W. Frontier of India, a very similar wild terrain, and with an equal amount of misplaced hope that dissident tribes could easily be brought to heel with a demonstration of air power. Most of both protectorates was peaceful but the wild men in the hills were more or less untouchable. Anyone who was operational in Aden knows that the contemporary hunt for Osama bin Laden is doomed to failure unless he is betrayed, the Afghan-Pakistan border being a carbon copy of the Upper Yaffa district in Aden. I have mentioned flag waves but we also dropped leaflets to tell residents of a village that so and so's house would be knocked down the next day. This triggered a standard response with the doors being taken off the house, as wood in South Arabia is scarce and valuable. The appointed hour would see most of the village guns ready for the first drive of the day – the arrival of the Venoms. Hundreds of rounds would be fired at each aircraft as it made its precision attack on the designated house and holes were frequent in our aircraft. At one stage our Squadron had 22 Venoms and in two days eighteen of them had small arms damage; if I hadn't seen it for real I wouldn't have believed that a jet aircraft could take as much punishment as they did without any effective damage.

One day they got lucky. Andy Devine and John Morris were knocking down a house at good old Al Qara when Andy heard "Red 2 I have been hit". Andy enquired as to whether John could finish the job with one more pass, assuming it was just the usual bullet hole, and was surprised to hear "Negative Lead, I have lost control of my engine and am bleeding quite a lot". A lucky round had come through the cockpit, severing the throttle and high-pressure cock control runs, and then passed through the top of his shoulder before stopping in his parachute. Luckily JM had 9000 RPM set and this was sufficient to clear the mountains and return to Khormaksar where he flew round and round until his fuel was exhausted. He was then able to carry out a flame out landing, as with no HP cock control, he was unable to shut down the engine; the LP cock was unusable by him as it was on the floor of the left-hand side of the cockpit and his bullet wound was in his left shoulder. Poor John, his luck did not last and he was killed at night over Cyprus in a Javelin when he collided with a Canberra. Andy, too, was shortly to die in a Hunter.

There were MIG-15s in the Yemen supposedly flown by the Ivans themselves but we never saw them. To be on the safe side though, when one of the old Vickers Valettas was doing a leaflet drop, a pair of fighters weaved above and behind them. This was necessary because the Venoms could not drop leaflets although, when the Hunters came, we stuffed leaflets into the airbrakes and selected them out when over the target area. The Valettas cruised at around 150 knots, the speed at which a Hunter left the ground, and not much above a Venom's stall so this was never a popular sortie. A jet aircraft is pretty safe at 400 knots as if anything should go wrong, the kinetic energy can be converted to height and height means time to sort out the problem or glide clear of angry Arabs if you have just knocked their house down. With the Venom we partially solved the problem by weaving over the Valetta at between 250 and 300 knots.

Sometimes the intelligence staff would tell a village that if they received arms from the Yemen they would be the centre of a proscribed area in which anything would be shot, including people and animals, the latter because they represented wealth and not because they were suspected of gun running. Flag waves, proscribed areas, leaflet drops and of course, occasionally, a little demolition were the control measures used, exactly as they had been on the NW frontier of India in the 1930s. When we were 'on ops.' flying was curtailed the day before to get the aircraft armed and serviceable and, when armed, each Venom had a red flag mounted on its nose so there was little secret about it. I did wonder, quite absurdly, about Nasser, the Squadron odd-job man who made the tea and coffee looked half starved and came from the Yemen. As a boy I had devoured all the Biggles books and remembered that in 'Biggles in the Orient' my hero uncovered a treacherous spy in the Officer's Mess called Lal Din who, when confronted by the great B, committed hari-kari all over the floor in the Officer's Mess ante room. I was reminded of the Oriental saga when Nasser was looking at the armed Venoms with flags and inquired "Tomorrow Operations yes?" "Yes", I replied, and was ashamed to think the thought that had briefly crossed my mind. A more unlikely spy would have been hard to find and the mess on the crew room floor would have to be cleared up by the junior pilot – still myself.

One day Andy Devine said that we were going to fly to Djibouti in French Somaliland for lunch. We took four Venoms and landed at noon for our goodwill visit; as I taxied in, I noticed three Junkers Ju52s, old WWII German transport aircraft, parked next to us. Even then in 1959 they looked incongruous antiques with their three radial engines and corrugated aluminium construction. I had never experienced French entertaining before. Lunch started at one and finished at four; I was very drunk without any doubt and the other three did not look much better. Our hosts drove us back to our Venoms where Andy found that they had not been refuelled and, worse still, that the drivers had finished for the day so – no fuel. After a short discussion, and bitterly regretting the use of the fuel during the impromptu four-ship formation we had flown on arrival, Andy said we could make it home without refuelling. We did, just. After take off we climbed straight ahead to 30,000' and did a long cruise descent back into Khormaksar during which I realised that if one had had too much, or much too much, vin rouge for lunch a transit from French Somaliland to Aden with very little fuel enabled one to sober up very quickly indeed.

Soon it was my turn to go 'up-country' again. I liked the phrase 'up-country', it certainly was the inverse of 'down-town' and so accurately described the translation from our life in Aden to the South Arabian hinterland. Soldiering in the Aden protectorates was run by the RAF regiment, with tanks and armoured cars supplied and usually crewed by the Army. What I saw of the 'RAF soldiers' was very good; I just could not quite understand why they were in the RAF. Upon my arrival at Ataq (appropriately enough pronounced 'attack') the Flight Lieutenant in charge of the operation the next day buttonholed me. "Ever been under fire?" he asked. "Only in my Venom", I replied. "Well, tomorrow you will find it a bit different when you are on the ground." I thought little of his remark until the next day. The master plan was for us to leave at dawn with some troops from the Aden Protectorate Levies, (Protectorate Arabs, British officered), in three lorries, three armoured cars and myself the ALO (air liaison officer, nowadays called an FAC or Forward Air Controller). We would drive to a local village at the foot of some hills, dropping off the lorries out of rifle range while the Ferrets and the ALO would drive forward to the village. I was then to call in the Venoms to do high-speed runs, the baddies would take to the hills and the Venoms would shoot them. The plan to me, even then, seemed a little naïve; it also had a major weakness. The APL troops would be safe in the rear; the regular army, who are paid to be killed, would be in their armoured cars, leaving only myself in an open top Land Rover exposed to hoards of angry Arabs armed to the teeth. (Arabs are always angry it seems, especially nowadays, just as they are always going to fight to the last drop of blood – inferentially their own – a loser mentality if ever there was one). The battle plan proceeded like clockwork. To start with we stopped the lorries a mile from the village and I and the three armoured cars drove forward.Someone must have been in charge, telling them to hold their fire because nothing happened until we halted at around four hundred yards when a hail of, mercifully, very badly aimed rounds came our way just as I had called in the first pair for a low run. I was amazed; as the Venoms turned in firing at us stopped and several hundred rounds were fired at the aircraft; as soon as the aircraft were clear firing resumed at us. I slowly became aware that 'us' meant me since my Arab driver had jumped out and fled behind a rock. None of that for me, I was British; I was, however, sitting bolt upright in my Land Rover clutching the microphone very tightly wearing my No.1 Service Dress hat and becoming aware that my mouth had gone very, very dry. Bullets were ricocheting off rocks making noises just like the films and then I felt one pass in front of my face, hearing the shot that fired it very soon afterwards. I decided to forgo my medal for conspicuous gallantry, and joined my Arab driver behind the rock. Half an hour later we all retreated, drove back to Ataq and I went back to Aden and the safety of my Venom cockpit. Being shot at in the air is a non-event but being shot at on the ground is a different ball game; I almost began to respect the Army's role in life.

One day Rex Knight, 'the boss', was in the crew room and being friendly. I should have been on my guard. "Have you ever thought of applying for a Permanent Commission, Tony?" he asked. I replied that I was certainly thinking about it and he invited me upstairs to his office. "It is very important for regular officers to have administrative experience" he began, "and as you know it is our turn to provide an adjutant at RAF Salalah in the Oman, so I am sending you, starting next week, to get some admin experience which will look good when you apply for a permanent commission." I was stunned, after six months I had become operational and was really happy, getting good scores on the range and loved the

Venom. Since leaving Chivenor I had had six months on Hunters in the Day Fighter role, six months on Transports, six months on Venoms as a Ground Attack Pilot and now I was to have six months as an adjutant on a small route station with no aeroplanes based there. I was not asked if I would volunteer, I was told I was going; was grounded immediately, and was to spend two days at HQ of the RAF at Steamer Point to learn about cyphers. I went to Cypher School, did not understand a word that I was being told about this very technical abstruse subject and took the Thursday Valetta transport for the route stations to RAF Salalah, just in the Oman, and six hundred miles from Aden.

Chapter 11

GROUNDED

Halfway along the coast line of Southern Arabia, and at the bottom south west corner of Oman, lay the small village of Salalah dominated by the palace of Sultan Said bin Taimur; at least it was a small village in 1959, but probably not now. As a location it was very unusual for Arabia as for several months of the year the coast was brushed by the same monsoon that provides so much rainfall in India.The Salalah coastal plain and low hills to the North then become alive with flowers and grasses. Had my soul not been left behind in Aden it would have been a really great tourist resort, particularly great because there were no tourists, and I could have enjoyed a six month sabbatical, with very little to do, amidst picturesque old Arab life, and stupendous swimming with my trusty mask and fins. The airfield was serviced by a BOAC subsidiary, Aden Airways, with Dakotas, or DC3s as they seem to be known nowadays, operating twice a week and, for the military, a bi-weekly service using Vickers Valettas, a twin engined, tail dragging, descendant of the Wellington. Both Aden Airways and the RAF operated a round trip taking two days to go from Aden to Mukalla to Salalah and then, after night stopping at Masirah, returning the next day. The Valettas brought some fresh food and mail, both much looked forward to. In the hills above Salalah was a huge cross visible from miles around, a monument to a transport crew caught out at the wrong place and the wrong height. No violent Islamic reaction in those days to the cross, a man's religion was his own affair; some Arabs prayed the regulation five times a day but many did not and no-one minded the giant cross.

I arrived by Valetta and was dropped in to RAF administration at the deep end. I had never even held a file until then but, on my first day, Sgt Fox came in with a pile of files for my signature. "What are all these for?" I enquired and I remember to this day his reply word for word. "Don't you worry about that Adj, you just sign and we will be all right." I just signed and kept on doing so for six months and we never had any trouble. Sgt Fox taught me how to decode signals using what looked like a typewriter operated by the German military, a system which had been 'broken' by Bletchley Park during the war. It did not seem a very secure method of sending 'secret' classified signals but then everything was 'secret' and virtually nothing important. One night after the great Fox had sent me solo on decryption I was dragged out of bed as a 'secret' signal that needed urgent decoding had just come in. Thinking at the very least that war must have been declared I ran to the signals section and was handed a piece of paper with rows of five figure groupings, which I finally decoded. The text read that, with effect from Xmas 1959, the entire Persian Gulf region of HM armed forces could expect a shortage of soap. I joke not and I am, even now, technically in breach of the official secrets act for having revealed this military crisis. I went back to bed not pleased. Sgt Fox had an amazing encyclopaedic knowledge; how to handle a cigar for instance. I had, most regrettably, started smoking cigars when Andy Devine, my Flight Commander at Khormaksar, had given me one to celebrate the birth of his second son, a habit he had inherited from the US Air Force during his time on Sabres in Korea. You should use one match to heat, evenly, the whole end and then a second match to ensure a smooth light up with no asymmetric burning, said Sgt Fox. After a few good puffs the band should be removed and never left on in English company although, in a few foreign countries, it was, apparently, a social gaffe to remove it. Sgt Fox recommended calling the British Embassy if I was in doubt when abroad. Where he found these gems I never discovered but he was always right.

RAF Salalah was just a hutted camp two miles north of the town and one of my jobs was to decode and deliver foreign office signals for the Sultan in his palace. One day I decoded one such and set off in the Landrover in my capacity as the Sultan's telegram boy; I parked neatly and set off on foot through the souk to the palace gates. Suddenly I was confronted by an elderly Arab who, after proffering all the usual greetings, grabbed me by the more private parts of my anatomy and clearly wished to get involved in a way that the love of my life had not. I felt a very serious diplomatic incident was about to take place as he would not let go and a curious crowd was beginning to gather. Then two of the Sultan's guards came to my rescue and, after I had delivered the urgent signal, they then escorted me back to my vehicle whilst two of their colleagues marched off my admirer.

There were two executive Officers at Salalah, the Officer Commanding and myself; we did nothing. There were eight senior NCOs who ran the whole place and around forty Junior NCOs and airmen who did all the work. I did not like the CO, a pompous little man and a navigator to boot; I had real problems having a navigator as my CO but then, shortly after I arrived, he went sick and I became 'the boss'. Luckily it was so obvious that I was very over-promoted for a 21-year-old Pilot Officer that the SNCOs rallied round and made sure everything ran smoothly for the week or two of the CO's absence. Occasionally very important people would arrive 'doing' the Middle East tour; I have a photograph of Field Marshal Slim, looking enormously fat, being welcomed to Salalah by the CO Pilot Officer (very slim then but now very fat) Haig-Thomas. Other visitors during my time as adjutant were David Stirling, founder of the SAS, who spent two nights in our tiny mess and Col Hugh Bousted, a life-long legendary Arabist who, when in London, had his bed taken to the roof of his Club as he could not sleep indoors. Other mess residents were Alf Manders, who liked bridge and fishing and was in the airfield construction branch, and Gerry and Kim whose surnames I forget and who were the civilian Clerks of Works; we also had a classic, dour, monosyllabic Scotsman who was the Air Traffic Controller (four movements a week). It might be thought that as a very immature twenty-one year old I might not get on very well with my much older mess mates but in fact I did and we had a very happy little outfit – especially when the CO was away.

One day I was in my office when the most senior NCO came in for a chat; he told me that he was leaving the RAF and retiring to Yorkshire to do nothing. "Won't you be bored?" I enquired. This brought forth his life story, in full detail, as time was not of the essence at Salalah, until finally he finished by saying that as aircrew he had been shot down, surviving two days in a dinghy until rescued by an RN destroyer. This had then been torpedoed and sunk and he had had several days in a lifeboat until rescued again. Finally he finished with the memorable line "so you see Adj, I have been everywhere, done everything and shagged everything so I think I shall put my feet up and do nothing." It was certainly some CV.

The Aden Airways DC-3 Captains provided good company when they stayed overnight - an objective opinion to show that I am actually quite flexible in my views on transport pilots. One of them played bridge and as we only had three players at Salalah he said he would fly up to Masirah Island, unload, and fly back on the same day, night-stopping with us. I forget the standard of his bridge but not his ability to drink whisky; he drank whisky all night. When it was time to take him down and help him into his aircraft early the next morning, it was already filled with blissfully unaware passengers. He then took off and flew west to Riyan and Aden. His departing words to me were "Don't worry old boy, I will have sobered up by the time I get to Aden". Another of his colleagues, just before I arrived, at a similar level of intoxication, had decided to liven things up a little on his departure with a 'beat-up' of the control tower; this he did a little tight with a full load of passengers and the wing tip hit the ground but caused only minor damage. On arrival back home at Khormaksar he reported hitting a gust on take off. I am sure he had sobered up when he arrived back at base even if his passengers needed a drink.

One day one of the DC-3 pilots who shared my passion for the sub-sea took me up to Masirah Island with him where he said the swimming was fantastic. The co-pilot liked snorkelling as well and kindly took a snooze while I logged a bit of DC-3 dual; when we arrived at Masirah the Captain took over and flew up and down a reef a couple of hundred metres off shore. "Look at those sharks" he said. I looked, and was thankful that we did not have to swim out there. After landing the Captain asked the Masirah CO to take us to his favourite beach for a little swim - it appeared to face out to the reef which had the very large black shapes swimming along it. To my consternation he then said we would swim out to that very reef to look at the beauty of the sharks in their natural environment; setting off from the beach the three of us had gone about forty metres when a shark started swimming round us. Our leader got our heads out of the water and shouted "Don't panic, we will attack". Ducking down he went straight for what, I now know, was a pretty harmless reef shark, which disappeared into the gloom. We swam on towards the reef and soon had two or three larger sharks swimming gently round us; readers who have come this far will know that I am completely fearless; however if I was to resume my flying career I needed to be alive, so I prompted our leader's head out of the water and said that I wanted to go home rather than face certain death. Behind the DC-3 Captain's head a fin appeared. "Off you go then," he said, "we are going to continue"; this was not what I had in mind. All the shark stories that I had read about involved being eaten while threshing around on the surface, so I took a deep breath, dived to the bottom, went as far as I could, and then went vertical for some air and back down again. I arrived on shore feeling a little embarrassed at my cowardice. When the other two eventually returned (to my amazement) I asked the co-pilot why he was so unafraid of being consumed alive, to which he replied that he was certain that I would not make it back in one piece alone and he had decided to die with his captain, not me.

Snorkelling was one of the great joys for me at Salalah. Once or twice a week I would take the Landrover and go ten miles to Risut and a little bay with a sandy beach and a steep shelf into water three or four feet deep; beyond the shelf was a coral field at depths between ten and twenty feet with mini-caves and coral overhangs. In the overhangs were huge numbers of crawfish which were just large lobsters without claws; the Arabs won't eat crawfish and no-one else at Salalah, or the American Oil Camp nearby, could be bothered so once or twice a week I would take a couple for my supper. I have always felt a little sorry for crabs and lobsters being boiled alive but I had read a letter in Country Life saying that lobsters placed head first into fresh water appeared to die instantly so I always took a large water container with me and it worked perfectly. One day I went to Risut and an enormous rock had appeared close in shore. It was only when I saw it move that I realised that it was a giant Manta Ray with two little ones either side of her tail, swimming very gently along the beach in the steep drop off, about two metres out. For a long time I watched this wonderful sight as they swam up and down the sandy shoal water, forgot my fishing and drove home. Actually catching a crawfish was too easy if you speared it so I used to grab them with one hand behind the head on the spiny carapace. Most times they escaped as I simply could not hold the thrust of their tails but I landed somewhere between one in five and one in seven and had them for dinner with some local bananas, Carnation milk and brown sugar; the latter concoction a life-long addiction. In the souk a whole hand of bananas could be bought for one shilling with sixty or seventy pieces of fruit on it; hung up, the fruit obligingly ripened in sequence from the bottom up but always stayed green even when ripe because, according to Sgt Fox, bananas would only go yellow in the dark. A shilling a hand may sound very cheap but it is the equivalent of around £1.50 today.

Life at this holiday resort soon settled into a pleasant routine. I ran the garden round our small mess which had paw-paw trees, banana plants, cotton bushes and other, to me, exotic plants. I went line fishing with Alf Manders and snorkelling, usually by myself. Sometimes I would look at the Myrrh and Frankincense bushes surrounding the old biblical ruins to the east of the town as this had been one of the start points for the ancient incense route of Arabia which had led, via the great Wadi Hadramaut to the Assir region, of what is now Saudi Arabia, and thence up the Hejaz mountain range to Shelley's 'Rose red city half as old as time', alias Petra, in today's Jordan.

Even further to the east was a large fresh water lake at Kerrure fed by streams from the hills and protected from the sea by a large sandbar. One day I organised a picnic for all those who wanted to go for lunch and a swim. We set off in the 'three tonner' lorry and, at the last moment, Sgt Fox decided to come. When we arrived I had just told everyone to have a swim before lunch when Sgt Fox rushed up and told me that I was mad as there were sharks in the lake and only a few years earlier an airman had lost a leg in quite shallow water. I did not believe him but, to be safe, stopped the swimming. Later I found out that an airman had indeed been attacked there and that there was a shark species that could survive in fresh water, to be specific the Bull Shark, a particularly aggressive version of this generally benign fish, at least as far as humans are concerned. I presumed that during a hurricane lots of salt water fish must have been washed over the sand bar into the fresh water lake, amongst which was the shark, or sharks; my letters home say that there were sting rays there too but I never saw one.

One day my happiness was destroyed by Al Withington leading a pair of Venoms and landing at Salalah. I remembered what I was meant to be doing in the RAF and it wasn't decoding signals, signing letters or growing papaya fruit. Al told me to apply to take any exam and have a few days back on the Squadron. I applied to take Mathematics and something called a General Paper as additional '0' levels as I had left school with only three of these and had failed Maths twice. It worked. I flew back to Aden, flew one Venom sortie by day and one by night and then was returned to Salalah. I passed on both papers. Times were changing on 8 Squadron; the Hunters were coming and I was away in the Oman far removed from the excitement and not very happy about it.

All the time I was in the RAF I was a regular correspondent with my family and my letters, or some of them, have survived. I have reproduced one of them as it captures the flavour of my life as an Adjutant and shows how I had, at the time, more or less forgotten about flying.

Sunday March 28th 1960
Royal Air Force, Salalah, BFPO 69

Dear Mum

Today I have been at Salalah for five months and it is only a month before I finish here. I do not have an exact departure date as it depends on how long Ken Brooking takes to be briefed on cyphers, accounting, catering and all the hundred and one duties one has to perform in an administrative role.

Rhamadhan has ended here tonight as we could see the moon, if you can't see the moon fasting must continue by day until you can see it. Up in Muscat it was cloudy so it is still on. This afternoon I went and took coffee with Hamood, a local sheikh - I have become his shooting partner, not because of my marksmanship but because I have access to a Landrover! Last week we went out after Gazelle (no luck) and ended up in the foothills at some caves at Gazes a few miles north of here where there is supposed to be an eighteen foot cobra, jet black, however we did not see it – thank heavens!

I went down to Aden and managed to get a couple of Venom trips and when I got back to Salalah Hamood had organised a guard of honour for me who fired their rifles low over my head in accordance with Arab tradition. The better the friend the closer go the bullets. It was the nearest thing I can imagine to a firing squad; however the CO was not pleased I think because, after he had commented on it, I made an unkind remark about his lack of communication with the locals.

Our Arab employees have given us a goat to eat, however, it is so nice we couldn't possibly kill it so we have christened it Charles and it is the new mess mascot as our tame gazelle has died of pneumonia. Not much more news, longing to see you all sometime during the summer.

Much love,
Tony.

My letter was wrong; my successor was a month late arriving so I arrived back on 8 Squadron at the end of May to find a big turnover of pilots and a squadron re-equipped with the Hunter.

Chapter 12

RHODESIAN ROMANCE

The Squadron was being sent to Rhodesia (I still cannot bring myself to write the word Zimbabwe); a deployment, via Nairobi, to Gwelo, a Royal Rhodesian Air Force station some three hundred miles south of Salisbury (I still cannot write the word Harare). Paralysis had set in as a great deal of work is involved in deploying an entire Fighter Squadron - including of course spares and engineers - some 2000 miles and so no-one was particularly interested in getting me airborne, except myself. 'Starry' Knight, the Squadron CO, had decided that I needed a dual check before I could fly a Hunter again and that, as I was out of practice, I should fly down to Rhodesia in a Beverley of 30 Squadron with the ground crew. I was elated as can be imagined.

Lots of new pilots were coming and old faces leaving, or had left, but among the new faces was John Volkers, a Cranwell graduate, who had made headlines throughout the UK as the competitor in the great London to Paris air race during which he had lost a little finger in a helicopter winch. John was great fun, quite irrepressible and hopeless with money – he always spent more than he had – but, in the short time he had been in Aden he had acquired a girlfriend at the very highest levels in the Colony. Well, the highest actually. As luck would have it she too had a girlfriend who had just arrived from England and was, let us just say, a very senior officer's daughter and so we made up a foursome. Colonel Briggs had heard that I was back from the dead and asked Volkers and me to lunch at Shuqra about 40 miles down the beach from Aden. When I say down the beach, I mean down the beach as the beach was the road. The four of us set off in John's car which, after around 20 miles, broke down leaving two young pilot officers with His Excellency's and the Air Commodore's daughters in the middle of nowhere and, much worse, likely to miss lunch. There appeared to be no traffic anywhere until at last an Arab lorry came swaying towards us, brightly coloured and piled high with goods of one sort or another; on top of the goods was the usual group of around a dozen Arabs who had hitched a lift. The lorry stopped and took us on board; John and I said we would avert our gaze as the girls climbed some ten feet up the ladder and then joined them; luckily one does not always have to keep one's word. We swayed along the beach, the Arabs chanted and sang, and eventually we drove into the army camp at Shuqra causing a stir when our transport, and travelling companions were seen; not a mode of transport expected for HE's daughter. After lunch the Colonel sent us back in a Land Rover and we towed John's car back to Khormaksar air base.

On June 1st 1960 Andy Devine, who was due to go home shortly, and had been posted to a ground job in the UK (as Flight Commander at a recruit school which must have pleased him), kindly asked John and me if we would join him and April for dinner. I had had a good day and at last flown two sorties in our twin seat Hunter with John Morris, so we much looked forward to a social evening with April and Andy. John and I arrived at 7.30 but Andy had not turned up as the Squadron had been night flying, so April gave us a couple of drinks and we waited. Suddenly there was a knock on the door and the Station Commander appeared; he said nothing to us, but John and I realising that this was not a social call, left at once. Andy was dead.

One of the new pilots, Mike Walley, had been having a dual night check and both he and Andy were used to flying the much higher performance Hunter FGA.9. They had climbed to what would have been 20,000', by time, in the Mk 9 single-seat aircraft but was in reality only 10,000' in the T.7. Aden nights are dark and altitude can in any case only be determined by reference to an altimeter. As I have mentioned elsewhere, misreading of altimeters by 10,000' was very common indeed in the Hunter era and came about due to the mismatch of power between the single-seaters, which were flown all the time, and the trainer version with the smaller 100 series Avon, flown very seldom. The standard let-down in those days was to home overhead at 20,000', be given an out-bound heading which was then followed by a steep descent to half the start height plus 2000'. Hunter T.7 XL615 started its descent and called "Turning left in-bound at 12,000'". A few seconds later there was a big flash in the desert as the aircraft buried itself in the sand and exploded. It had actually been at 2000' when it started its turn, and not 12,000'.

I flew a few sorties including one up to Sharjah in the Persian Gulf; turning overhead Salalah at 40,000'; I almost felt nostalgic. It was the first time I had flown a Hunter with four underwing tanks, 2 x 230 gallons on the in-board stations and 2 x 100 on the out-board. The aircraft was very heavy; our initial climb was to 36,000' where at that weight and Mach.85 the aircraft was very close to the Mach stall in any manoeuvre and after a slightly rough pitch input I fell 2000' before I got things back under control. It took 100 out of our 2 x 100 gallons to carry the other 100 gallons to a point where it could be used – an example of how the law of diminishing returns applies to aircraft as well as to other areas of economics.

The Squadron finally left for Rhodesia. I and two other pilots left in the Beverley in a poor state of mind as we droned down to Nairobi at 145 knots instead of 550. I heard later that the Squadron had a near miss. When they should have been able to talk to Nairobi, there was no answer; an unforecast wind had blown them well off course and nearly out of radio range. Dennis Hazell the new 'B' Flight Commander, flying at one extreme side of the spread-out tactical formation could only just receive the tower transmissions, thereby saving the Squadron from a total loss. It was almost unbelievable, even then, to put into service a tactical fighter Squadron which had no means of navigation beyond 180-200 miles. Every American fighter carried an ADF, as did every commercial airliner, but the RAF decided not to fit their fighter aircraft with one so a flight to Nairobi had to be carried out at 40,000' with no navigational aids for 70% of the flight. Sadly Dennis Hazell was to die in a Gnat while flying with the Red Arrows a few years later when he collided with Euan Perreaux, another of our new pilots, doing the Arrows head on cross over, normally flown with a small lateral displacement.

Eventually the Hunters and the Beverley arrived at Gwelo; our African maps of the 1950s had half the second leg marked 'unexplored swamp' – not a good place to eject. The Rhodesian Air Force were very hospitable. I flew two or three local sorties during which I found that, having the sun in the wrong place, since we were south of the equator, made me very disoriented. After my third sortie the weekend had arrived and Volkers and I needed a little action on the love front while the rest of the Squadron drank beer. I had had several chats with a young Rhodesian Air Force pilot, David Thorne, later chief of the Rhodesian Air Force, and I explained our urgent requirements. After a little thought he nominated two sisters who he felt should help alleviate our problem but they were in Salisbury a hundred and fifty miles away. Ever helpful he drove us there, introduced us to the girls and then went on his way; the boss had said that he wanted a pair of Hunters that were at Salisbury Airport brought down to Gwelo on Monday and thus the scene was set for the great disaster triggered by that heady mix of jets and girls and 21-year old boys. We took the girls to a dinner dance at Meikles Hotel and after a bit I asked mine, the elder of the two, and, as I kept telling John, much the prettiest, if she would like to dance. She said she would so long as it was at arms length. She said that if people wanted to dance they should dance and if they wanted to make love they should make love, but they should never try and mix the two. I agreed and felt weak at the knees. We saw little of Salisbury that weekend but the girls' brother had popped in and said that he would have liked to have seen the Hunters on Monday, but that he had to work at the Caltex building in Salisbury. John said that that was no problem; we would give him a fly by, which was how the great disaster started.

On Monday morning July 18th, 1960, the girls drove John and I out to Salisbury Airport; the weather was as good as it gets for flying and in Africa that is very good indeed with unlimited visibility and traditional fluffy cumulus five or six thousand feet above ground level. We had kisses goodbye and then, endeavouring to look as casual as possible, climbed into the Hunters. The girls were told to stand by the wing opposite the cockpits so that they could get the maximum effect of the initial purge and firing of our 'isopropyl nitrate' starters which are awe-inspiring, should you be close and not have seen it happen before. The girls promised to wave us goodbye and we promised them a flypast if they did. Trouble was coming to the boil in the witches' cauldron.

'Snowstorm Black' was our call sign and we did a 'pairs' close-formation take-off which, with our thrust reduced by the 5000' altitude and heat of that part of Africa, took longer than usual; John had won the toss and was leading so when our wheels left the ground I touched the brakes to stop the main tyres rotating into the wheel bay, and, with my left hand, pushed the 'up' button to retract the undercarriage. As the lead Hunter started its turn to the right I slid down and under it before moving out into a low level tactical position from which I would have complete freedom of manoeuvre. The tower gave us clearance for a fly-by and, as we turned in, I noticed that I had .9 on the Mach meter. A fly-by in any jet at .9 is always impressive, not because of the speed but because it comes at you silently until there is an apocalyptic explosion of sound. I never saw the girls waving, as I was wondering if John was going to hit the ground, never having seen a jet as low as his was other than when landing. Time to show the girls' brother the sort of thing that his sisters' lovers were made of. The Pearl Assurance building dominated the Salisbury skyline and, using it as a marker, we entered a long gentle curve from the airport to line up with the palm trees that lined Kingsway at the end of which lay the Caltex building where the girls' brother worked. We flashed past at the same height as the top of the building – well only a little bit below – still at .9M which probably wasn't a good idea, but, perversely, I was only concerned with a bird-strike and the unthinkable damage that would be done by a Hunter full of fuel at .9 impacting in the middle of a city after I had ejected. The birds stayed away.

There is a railway that runs between Salisbury and Bulawayo and half way along it lay Gwelo with the Royal Rhodesian Air Force base of Thornhill next to it. Leaving Salisbury John turned south west to pick up the line still with .9 on the Mach Meter, while I moved over to a position on his left with the railway line running between us. In the distance I saw a train coming, puffing its tell tale cloud of smoke and steam across the African Veld. As we passed it, however, the driver was subjected to a stereophonic explosion and, since he had not seen our approach, assumed an engineering catastrophe and did an emergency stop. I am ignorant of steam technology but the RAF were informed that he had 'squared off' his wheels and were sent a bill for a new set. I imagine that 'squared off' meant a flat spot which would feel very unbalanced at anything other than low speed. Soon a small town appeared ahead. John did seem very low as we passed it, while I was using the No.2's privilege of flying a comfortable position about 100 yards back and 100 feet up, displaced laterally by about 200 yards. I seem to remember that the small town was called Hartley and it was bad luck that nineteen windows in a girls' school shattered as we went past, but of course we did not know that at the time. After Hartley, John pulled up to 25,000'. I moved wide into a high level 'battle' position, around 1000 yards on his left and sat in motionless silence wondering as ever at the beauty of the Hunter and the silence of jet flight. Suddenly

John's voice broke my reverie. "I've got a hard on" it said. Whatever could he mean? Perhaps it was a warning of some technical failure or other. The man was incorrigible and anyway we couldn't turn back to Salisbury now to get it fixed. We landed, taxied in, shut down and wandered into the Squadron; so young, stupid and naive that I for one had put the whole episode out of my mind. John and I were each enjoying a coffee when the Boss's office door opened. "Tony, John, can you come here a second". We went in, the Boss was smiling. "Have you two been naughty boys?" We owned up and those were the only recriminatory words he ever said, but far worse was to come.

The full might of the RAF legal system now swung into action. The Wing Commander Flying at Khormaksar had flown down in a support Beverley on a 'jolly' and he was assigned the task of taking a 'Summary of Evidence' which is a legal requirement before a Court Martial. Things were not looking good for John's career. Having been an outstanding Cranwell cadet with Air Marshal written all over him, it looked as though he would have to retire as a Pilot Officer whereas I had at least just been promoted to Flying Officer and was only doing a total of eight years anyway. The Wing Commander took formal statements from us and then he, Mike Russell (another 8 Squadron pilot), and John and I drove to Hartley to hear various witnesses describe what they had seen. Things did not sound too good until the headmistress came in, and then they sounded much worse. She had been standing on her dining room table apparently doing some dusting, when a Jet Fighter flew past the window at the same height as her; this definitely sounded as if we were guilty. The Wing Commander was busy writing this down; Mike Russell sat on his right while John and I sat behind Mike; the door opened and in came the school gardener. He had been in the RAF during the war and the Wing Commander established that he would consider himself an expert witness. "Now, how high would you say these jets were?" The gardener paused; John and I raised the palms of our hands rapidly up and down finishing with prayer palms pressed together. The gardener appeared to be thinking, taking his time as befits a professional witness. "About 1500 feet" he said. The Wing Commander looked surprised, questioned the height, received a positive confirmation and closed the meeting. On the way back to Thornhill in the car he suddenly announced that he had exceptionally good peripheral vision. Whatever could he have meant?

John and myself, under arrest and escorted by Wing Commander Bower and

Mike Russell, were sent back to Aden in a returning support Beverley. Mike was the escorting officer, in case we tried to make a run for it and, after a very noisy seven or eight hours, we arrived at Nairobi. Unsurprisingly there were no friends in the Beverley crew so the four of us left them drinking beer at Embakasi and took a taxi into town where we spent a very agreeable evening at the Equator Club, at the time Nairobi's best night club. We went to bed very late, and with only a few hours in bed the four of us enjoyed an anaesthetised sleep back to Aden; at last I had found a way to minimise the full horror of travel in an RAF Beverley.

Back in Aden we were grounded; to our peer group and the rest of the colony our escapade ensured our notoriety and many invitations to parties. The story told and re-told bore little resemblance to the facts (for the record we were not inverted past the Caltex building). When the signal had arrived at RAF HQ, Steamer Point, informing them of a flagrant breach of low flying regulations but without naming the pilots, the SASO (Senior Air Staff Officer) told the AOC that it was bound to be Haig-Thomas and Volkers, a libellous slur on our reputations, but our invitations to dinner at Steamer Point where the hierarchy lived dried up. The case for the prosecution was sent to the Air Ministry where a recommendation for Court Martial was made. At this juncture many friends helped out; it was decided by the AOC that to fly the witnesses up from Rhodesia was too expensive and that he would deal with it himself. John and I were summoned to HQ and I, absolutely petrified, was ushered in to Air Vice Marshal David Lee's office; my mouth went dry and I spent the interview struggling to prevent myself laughing. This must have been an interesting psychological reaction brought on by nerves. I found nothing funny in the proceedings, quite the reverse; I was terrified. After a very one-sided interview he announced that I would lose six months seniority and I was dismissed. At last I held some sort of RAF record; I had only been a Flying Officer for two months but now I was a Flying Officer with minus four months' seniority. John became an even more junior Pilot Officer by six months and we went back to Khormaksar to join the land of the living as fully restored Squadron pilots. We were never restored to social acceptance amongst the more senior members of the RAF at HQ, and the dinner invitations dried up, but the 11th Hussars had arrived in Little Aden with many of my school friends and acquaintances among them so we exchanged one social life for another.

The intervention of senior officers to protect junior ones under their command was one of the better features of RAF life and John and I were not alone. My Flight Commander was now 'Porky' Munro and one day he lost his revolver while 'up-country' with the army. Losing a weapon is an automatic court martial offence however, as soon as Group Captain John Merrifield DSO etc etc heard of it 'Porky' was summoned to station HQ and fined £5. When the evidence was sent to Command HQ the matter had to be dropped as he had already been punished; I heard later that the Group Captain was told that he had acted beyond his powers but he knew that, as he had implied as much when issuing his fine.

Shortly after our rehabilitation, the Boss told me that I could have my name written under the cockpit of Hunter 'Q'. Soon it appeared and I had my photograph taken in full flying kit with my name clearly showing and, as my love life had dried up, I sent it to the love of my life hoping to rekindle some interest when I returned to the UK so alas I have no copy of it, and, worse, it did not even have the desired effect. Four days later Les Swain flying 'Q' hit a rock doing 500 knots in the Upper Yaffa and my aircraft was no more and neither was Les. Les had arrived on the Squadron just before I left for Salalah and I had sold my little Fiat 500 car to him for £150 which I had originally purchased for £100, to this I had added £100 of savings and proceeded to purchase 300 shares in Minet Holdings at 18s.6d a share (90p). Minet Holdings did very well and I more than trebled my money in a very few months. After Les was killed I bought the Fiat back for £100. Most satisfactory; a profit of six months salary, clean of tax, to compensate for no flying for six months.

My flying now had a hiccup. The new 'wheels' in the Squadron were my friends from the Meteor flight but I had trouble coming to terms with their methodology of low-level navigation. There was nothing clever about it but I developed a complex which meant that something fundamentally easy became a major problem. Manx Kelly was assigned to be my personal mentor and after about six weeks he and I had it 'sorted' to use a contemporary expression. Although I could navigate at high speed and low level I was never that good at it but, back on the range, my Hunter scores were equal to, and eventually better than, those of my Venom days.

Chapter 13

BACK ON THE SQUADRON

Volks and I settled back into the normal existence of a young pilot on a fighter squadron. It was August 1960 and our stupid – with hindsight – low flying episode forgotten by all except the flight Commanders who remained very disapproving. The Hunters however failed to oblige and day after day went by with one and occasionally two aircraft serviceable; life was miserable and morale very low. I flew three and a half Hunter hours in August and then the Squadron was grounded as our two engineers tried to get to grips with the mass unserviceability. I then flew no Hunter trips until November 15th and it was only because I could fly, and was rated on, the Meteor that I flew at all; even so eleven hours in the Meteor and none in a Hunter in two and a half months on a Hunter Squadron did not make for much happiness. One day I was walking over to the main mess building to see 'Stack' Butterley from my old Jet Provost days ('Stack' was on the Shackleton Squadron although he later became a Concorde captain). I started walking up the stairs to his room when, suddenly, I felt so weak that I could go no further and sat down. I felt that I was dying. Then a thought occurred to me that perhaps I needed salt; I made it into the mess dining room and ate half a dozen salt tablets and a miracle occurred. Within two minutes I felt better and after five I walked out as fit as ever; I knew we needed salt over and above that normally consumed because of the colossal sweat rates in the Aden hot season but had always eschewed the salt tablets. Never again.

To raise morale it was decided to hold an 8 Squadron ball at Khormaksar; anyone who was anyone in the colony was invited and it certainly kept everyone busy for a fortnight. Manx Kelly painted on frames some huge murals of 8 Squadron aircraft from the thirties, and John Volkers and I were put in charge of the catering but with a pitifully small budget. The food would have been quite inadequate so we decided to overspend our budget by £100; another disaster. The boss was furious and, although he never admonished us for our low flying, he made it clear that I was useless if I could not even control a limited budget - ironically one of the few things that I am good at, but I did not feel inclined to say that it had been deliberate. The ball was a huge success and the food lavishly praised, especially the trout and avocados flown in from Kenya in a Beverley.

Keeping bored pilots busy is a hard task, especially in a place like Aden, so my Flight Commander 'Porky' Munro decided that 'B' Flight would have a dinghy drill. He booked an RAF Air Sea Rescue launch and nine of us set sail from the Aden Harbour on a beautiful still day; the sea was the proverbial mirror reflecting the azure blue sky. About five miles out from Aden the launch stopped and we got ourselves ready to jump overboard but, when we were ready, it was very apparent that we had company as there were three or four large sharks swimming round and round the boat. Clearly there were no volunteers to start the exercise but after about fifteen minutes of fish watching, the sharks just disappeared, fed up with waiting for the scraps of food that often are thrown from ships. 'Porky' decided that it was time to get our drill underway, only to be faced with 'insubordination', 'mutiny', 'failing to carry out an order from a superior officer', all in good humour. Finally he said he would be first in. He took a flying leap into the sea while we all watched from the launch; we saw him inflate his Mae West and dinghy, then climb into the dinghy and lie there in the sun, dangling his arms and legs in the water and urging us to join him. Suddenly about twenty yards from him, and behind his head, emerged a huge triangular fin heading straight for his very small, inflatable, one man rubber boat. A pantomime scene followed with us all shouting "look behind you" and a relaxed Munro saying "Yes, yes, I am not falling for that one." When he did look behind him and saw what was heading straight for him the look on his face was unforgettable – it will remain with me forever. The shark glided past his little dinghy and we recovered our fearless, but rather white around the gills, Flight Commander as quickly as possible, who then declared that dinghy was drill completed. As we turned homeward, and before the launch had opened up a Marlin leaped out of the water with its sail erect and its long spiked nose giving it its classic shape. A beautiful sight.

One day Brian Griffith and Mick Murden, our engineer officers, got the Hunters flying again and all our miseries faded away. I was briefed to take two Hunters up to Bahrain and bring two very tired aircraft back to Aden, refuelling at Sharjah each way. It was one of my more memorable flights. Tim Seabrook flew as my No.2 and we arrived at Bahrain and night stopped. The next day, fully fuelled, we left for Sharjah and, having more fuel than we needed, flew low-level to burn it off. All RAF low level sorties are flown at 420, 480 or 540 knots representing 6, 7 or 8 nautical miles a minute. I went for 480 in crystal clear conditions at 4000'. Qatar appeared, looking exactly like the map and we passed across its northern tip. Whenever I see a map of the Persian Gulf today I remember that sortie. We landed at Sharjah, refuelled, and departed high level for the nearly 1000-mile flight to Aden via overhead Salalah and thence down the coast 600 miles to Aden. We settled into the high level cruise over the great rolling red sand dunes of the empty quarter of Arabia. It is called the Empty Quarter because there is nothing, absolutely nothing, there and I sat marvelling at the silence and beauty of the scene with Tim a mile line abreast of me. Suddenly, in my headset, I heard a click, just that, a tiny electronic click. Thinking it might be a 'dolls eye' magnetic indicator on the fuel panel I glanced down and saw to my horror that I had lost transfer pressure from my right hand fuel tanks; worse still, as I looked, there was another click and the left hand dolls eye showed a left hand fuel failure. I had 1300lbs of usable fuel in the main collector tanks until I flamed out and then I was dead. I pressed the transmit button "Hey, Tim, I have just had a double transfer failure". Back came the words forever etched in my mind, "Sooner you than me, mate". There was nothing I could do except wait for the flame extinction followed by my own, from thirst, a couple of days later in those great red rolling sand dunes. Tim said nothing and then with my fuel down to 600 lbs I heard another click, the right hand fuel system started pumping fuel back into my main fuselage tank, then it failed again. Then the left side started feeding and I flew back to Aden with a stream of transfer failures and recoveries. When I got home the engineers said that there was insufficient pressure to transfer any fuel and were surprised that I made it.So was I.

Shortly after my return, the Navy arrived. I forget which carrier it was, but the Sea Hawks flew into Khormaksar led by Lt. Cdr Noble and shared our crew room. I really wanted to fly one and decided to ask him if I could on the grounds of nothing ventured, nothing gained; unsurprisingly he said 'no' but he added that he was going to become Commander Air at Lossiemouth on his return and if I got myself there he would let me fly a

Sea Hawk. I was elated. Lt. Cdr. Noble had been a test pilot at Farnborough and unveiled many mysteries of supersonic flight; for example that unstable vortices developed on the nose of an aircraft when supersonic, switching from one side to the other, which could lead to dangerous directional instability at High Mach numbers; that the skin temperature could be determined by use of the simple formula True Air Speed over 100 squared; the mysteries of roll yaw coupling in aircraft at high angles of attack with the mass concentrated in the fuselage leading to tumbling and structural failure. I was hooked, and decided that Test Pilots' School was where I was headed.

During this time minor political troubles erupted, leading to minor military operations. An area had been proscribed west of Ataq due to bad behaviour by the locals. I was leading a pair and the proscription seemed to be working – there was not a camel, goat or man to be seen. Then, right in front of me, was a camel. I turned hard left through 360°; my No.2 following, sighted on the camel and touched the gun button; as soon as I had fired I pulled up and round to see what had happened. The camel was nowhere to be seen, and then I saw a huge red circle where the camel had been and now wasn't. That big red circle has remained with my conscience ever since. On another occasion there had been trouble at Al Qara, again, and Manx Kelly and I were briefed to knock down a house. Leaflets had been dropped the day before to avoid human casualties, the wooden doors removed to avoid financial loss, and the village guns lined up to enjoy the sport. Until around ten o'clock there is little wind in up-country Arabia, making it ideal for a gun attack, as our trusty rockets were not accurate enough to guarantee precision work. Manx and I got airborne and headed north eventually swinging into a large fast orbit to ensure that we had identified the correct house. Once satisfied, Manx turned in but just as he was about to fire, a great ball of white appeared from behind his aircraft followed by a long white trail stretching for a mile behind. I called "Red lead you have been hit", and found that he had had no idea. I tucked up in close formation and saw that the whole of the back end of his right hand drop tank was missing but no other damage. The white trail was fuel being sucked out of his wing tanks. Manx said that we would finish the job with one pass, turned in again followed by me at around a mile not wishing to put my gun sight on my leader. Manx had fired-out so I put the fixed cross well above the house to allow for the gravity drop at extreme range, assumed no wind, and dumped a full war load in one pass, and was enormously pleased and slightly surprised to see my rounds on the target. Manx called me to rejoin and we headed south; suddenly he called me into close formation and accelerated, then, applying G., he pulled into a loop, then another one and then a barrel roll. I had flown my first formation aerobatics while staring at a big black hole that was all that was left of my leader's 230 gallon tank.

Soon after this sortie I had one of those incidental experiences that I suspect all pilots have from time to time. They are of no significance in themselves; they are of a fleeting nature but then leave an indelible print in the mind. I was doing a solo high level sortie for some reason or another -solo sorties are rare occurrences in the single seat world - and I was flying east about ten miles off-shore when on my right hand side I noticed a line on the ocean as straight as it is possible to get, stretching from underneath my Hunter to the coast of Somalia nearly a hundred miles away. Ever curious as to its cause, I raised the nose of my aircraft and rolled it inverted; immediately below me was a giant super-tanker ploughing eastwards, and I had seen its bow wave, or rather the shadow of its bow wave, showing up very black on the brightly lit ocean. It is an interesting thought that if, when paddling on the beach with your trousers rolled up to the knee and a knotted handkerchief on your head, you get soaked by a much larger than usual wave, it could be caused by a ship completely out of sight.

We worked very closely with the army and soon it was decided to hold some exercises during which I very nearly killed myself. I had been briefed to look for troops hiding in one of the Wadis west of Aden and, if we spotted any tanks from the Queen's Own Hussars, to do a simulated gun attack on them. We strapped in, fired up and started pounding up and down the Wadis. I thought it ridiculous as we would never spot a battalion, let alone a platoon that was well hidden. And then I saw it; out of the corner of my eye I saw a man's head look up at me – had he not moved I would never have seen it but in wartime a simple tiny act of indiscipline would have ensured his and his colleagues' deaths. I pulled off, marked the spot on my map for debrief, and headed west with my No.2 looking for tanks and there they were, two lovely big tanks. With the gun sight set I turned in on the leader, achieved a perfect sight setting and pressed the cine button rather than the trigger in order to preserve good relations between the Army and the RAF. Releasing the button I raised the nose and then had a perfect sight on the second tank but by now I was very low and fast; I touched the cine button again then pulled as hard as I dared up to 7G, the Hunter's nose came up well but the aircraft's inertia caused it to continue its downward path. The desert came up round my ears and I just had time to think, "Christ, I have had it" when I hadn't. The ground fell away beneath me and no one ever knew that I had killed myself through stupidity but got away with it. That weekend I met one of the Queens Own Hussars at a party who had been in the second tank and had not been pleased to be sand blasted by my jet wake and, then, I thought nothing further of the incident until a few days later when I suddenly had a very bad night as the reality of what I had done struck home.

Several new pilots had arrived on the Squadron. Ken Hayr, who I had met at Acklington on 66 Squadron was one. A graduate of Cranwell, we were chalk and cheese and good friends until he died at the Biggin Hill Air Show in a Vampire in 2000; Ken had Air Marshal written all over him and was a stickler for everything being very correct. In Aden at the time, uniform was shorts, shirts, long stockings and black shoes; it was permissible, however, to wear long trousers and desert boots but with black socks. Amongst the smarter military set fashion had moved to very dark red socks and Ken spotted me wearing these one day and gave me a good talking to about uniform conformity. Two days later the SASO, Air Commodore de la Poer-Beresford came to visit the Squadron, himself a former very distinguished ground attack pilot from el Alamein, and sat on the table to talk to us, idly swinging his legs, and there, to my enormous joy, not only were there glimpses of red socks but Ken Hayr had noticed. From then on I was left in peace and Ken went on to become an Air Marshal in black socks.

When the convoys were running to and from Dhala seventy miles north of us we had to have a pair of armed Hunters on standby from first light at six o'clock. One day it was my turn as No.2 to my Flight Commander Porky Munro. I arrived early and, with the ground crew, prepared both aircraft for flight; of PM there was no sign, not that it mattered, as Dhala convoys were seldom shot at these days. At 6.15 the crew-room door opened and there was my leader for today's standby pair very, very much the worse for no sleep at all, sexual excess and a great deal of his favourite tipple. At that very moment the telephone rang to say that the army had been ambushed and needed close air support. I told PM to pretend that his aircraft wouldn't start and was in turn told to mind my own business. To my horror we got airborne and at 500 knots very quickly found the convoy with both of us dumping a full war load of 30mm where the baddies were supposed to be – Porky was brilliant, his leading and gun attack perfect, his RT crisp and purposeful and the convoy rolled forward as we pulled off and headed south. Suddenly I was called into close formation and P announced 'loop loop go' and off we went for my second formation aerobatic lesson but this time with a very drunk lead who was as smooth as silk. Soon we landed back at Khormaksar to find the boss, still Sqn. Ldr. 'Starry' Knight waiting as, having heard the early morning scramble, he wanted to know what had happened; he then asked us back to breakfast with his wife 'Wiz'. Breakfast went well with my esteemed leader trying not to slur his words but I wondered about his health when the double fried egg appeared. Eventually the ordeal was over and we drove off; Porky said 'Wiz' was not getting enough but I could not work out what on earth he meant. Tales from Porky's and Manx's Swift days in Germany were legion. One night they had failed to get to bed and arrived at 79 Squadron still in their dinner jackets and very well oiled. As a gimmick they were allowed to fly the first sortie of the day in their DJs and all went well until a blocked runway at Gütersloh caused a diversion to a nearby USAF air base. As the Swifts shut down and the hoods motored back the USAF were surprised to see two 'gentlemen' in dinner jackets emerge from each cockpit. It could have been a cut from a James Bond film except that none had, by then been filmed.

As a mobile tactical squadron 8 Squadron had a full time, non-flying adjutant, Barry Wylam. Barry had just bought a new camera and wanted a film of a Hunter going low and fast. For some reason or other he thought of me when he saw I was doing an air test one afternoon. Barry and his wife Angela went up to the top of the tower and I was cleared for a .9 run down the airfield at 500'. On completing the tests I duly obliged, pitching out of the run into the downwind position from which I landed, taxied in and shut down. Walking back to sign the paper work I found

"A" Flight - No.82 Course, RAF Kirton-in-Lindsey, March 1956.
Back Row: Ashmore, Ashwood, Baldwin, Cassidy, Checkley, Cockburn.
Centre Row: Corrans, Cumming, Downes, Freeman, Geaves, Gregory.
Front Row: Gregg, Grindon, Haig-Thomas, Hassall, Heron.

No.116 Course, No.8 FTS, RAF Swinderby, November 1957. Three stayed in the RAF.
Don Betts flew Canberras for nearly 30 years, Jim Baldwin became a Vulcan
captain and Chris Gould became a Group Captain.

The Percival Provost T.1. The author flew 30 hours on the Piston Provost just before he left the RAF. A lovely handling aircraft.

Only ten Hunting Jet Provost T.1s were produced and XD693 is the only airworthy example.

The main equipment of No.8 FTS was the de Havilland Vampire FB.5 and T.11. Dual was flown in the T.11s and most soloed in the FB.5. The author flew this particular aircraft at Swinderby in 1957 and was still flying the same aircraft fifty years later. WZ507 (G-VTII) operated by the Vampire Preservation Group is pictured during a sedate flypast at Old Warden in 2007. *(Jarrod Cotter/Key Publishing)*

The Supermarine Swift F.7 as used by the Guided Weapons Development Unit stationed at RAF Valley. The best of the breed, but to late to enter squadron service. An object of the authors desire; this type eluded him.

Beautiful clean lines of the Hawker Hunter F.4 as operated by No.229 OCU at RAF Chivenor. The author flew these low powered variants with 100 series Avons producing 7500lbs against the 10,000lbs in the F.6.

Three Junior Pilots. The three junior pilots of No.63(F) Squadron at RAF Waterbeach, Cambs. From the left; Mike Seymour, Trevor Phillips and AHT aged 20. A certain lack of respect is being shown by our squadron colleagues. Seymour became a solicitor and Phillips President of BALPA the airline pilots union.

Hawker Hunter F.6 of 66 Sqn based at RAF Acklington.

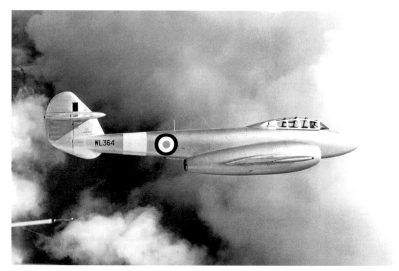

WL364. The author checked out on the Gloster Meteor T.7 while on his first Hunter squadron. He eventually logged 600 hours on the type.

The Meteor F.8 was the definitive fighter variant and heaven to fly.

The Meteor NF.14 flew like a Canberra. The author scrounged a flight with 25 Squadron at Waterbeach.

I found the Canberra T.4 a lovely, easy aircraft to fly.

An extra seat in the Hunter did little to upset the clean lines of the Hunter T.7.

Tony (Left) en route to Aden May 1959 aged 21, taken in Kano, Nigeria and Ollie Sutton (Right) Ollie became editor of Air International in Geneva and was an old friend from Ludgrove and Eton. Here he is in the Royal Rhodesian Air Force.

Fg Off Alan Withington poses in the cockpit of his 8 Squadron Venom at Salalah in January 1960.

8 Sqn Venom at Salalah in 1960. The author flew the Venom again forty years later.

A pair of 8 Squadron Venoms, RAF Salalah, Oman where the author spent six months, prepare for take off in January 1960; Cpl Baldock watching.

The author climbs aboard a Meteor T.7 of the Arabian Peninsular Reconnaissance Flight at RAF Riyan near Mukalla 300 miles from Aden along the South Arabian Littoral. The aircraft had been borrowed for a few days while Michael Murden and the author explored the Wadi Hadramaut.

Far too much time was spent on the ground to Air Radio and not enough flying.

In Wadi Sayeed hoping not to be shot or killed by the various deadly species of wild life that shared our fort.

Forward Air Controller on a Dahla convoy. The author was trying to look like Rommel.

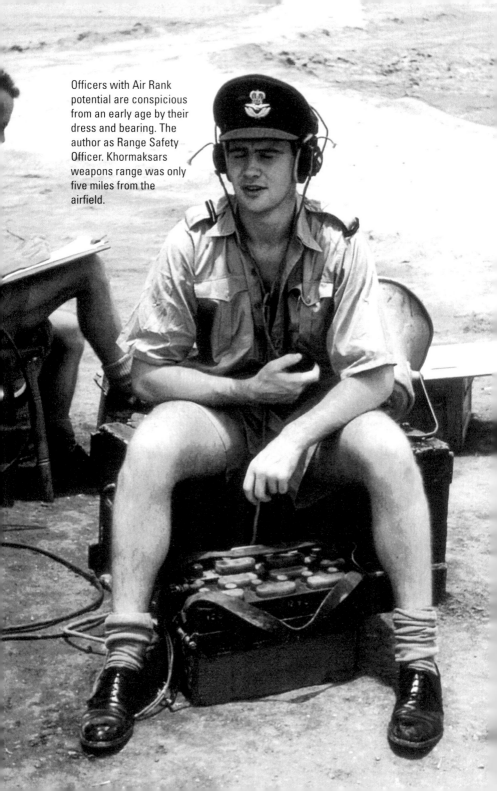

Officers with Air Rank potential are conspicious from an early age by their dress and bearing. The author as Range Safety Officer. Khormaksars weapons range was only five miles from the airfield.

Dinner at the Government Guest House in the Wadi Hadramaut. A 'Jolly' with Mike Murden the squadron Engineering Officer.

Girls were in short supply in Aden. Unknown Army Officer left, the author and Barry Wylam 8 Squadrons Adjutant and Old Radleian. He got me six days orderly officer by getting me to do a .9M run down Khormaksars runway one afternoon.

Left to right; the author, Group Capt P O V Green and Air Vice Marshal Gareth Clayton my boss and long-term friend.

AOCs Inspection at RAF Chivenor in the summer of 1962. ADC showing off executive clipboard and golden aiguillettes.

Gloster Javelin T.3 (above) of 33 Squadron and (below) a Javelin FAW.9 from the same unit. The Mk.9 Javelin was flown with 33 Squadron by the kindness of the CO Wg Cdr Caryl Gordon The Duke of Edinburgh's old instructor.

K XH692

The author was the last student through 228 OCU at RAF Leeming, Yorkshire. He flew the T.3, FAW.5 and FAW.9 with the big engines. The conversion was done after the Squadron Leader at 11 Group HQ had forbidden it.

The glorious Hunter F.6. The author flew the type on 63 and 8 Squadron but scrounged flying from 19, 92 and 66 Squadron as well. He flew the type for fourteen months in Saudi Arabia.

Gloster Meteor T.7 bird strike on the 4th September 1963. Note feathers coming out of the wing through the rivet heads. The bent aileron rods visible in lower picture gave very restricted roll control. The author had lost his air speed indicator and was very short of fuel.

Everyone has a low point in their flying career. For the author, it was six months on 242 TCU at RAF Dishforth in Yorkshire and over 92 hours as second pilot on the Handley Page Hastings.

Tiger Club Tribute to Sir Geoffrey de Havilland during the Memorial Service at St Albans Abbey 21st July 1965. Clive Francis was a former CO of 54(F) Squadron, John Thomson became C-in-C Strike Command and Martin Barraclough edited this book. Arriving at Hatfield in torrential rain Martin just missed the Hatfield ILS mast, the author flew straight into it and Neil Williams just missed the wreckage. A spare Tiger was borrowed for the occasion.

Redhill 1965, Jodel D150 Masceret Pre take off for France, Spain and Morocco with David Buik. Two days later I nearly killed us both. Buik is now to be heard and seen on radio and TV as one of the BBC's city commentators.

Self flying Cosmic Wind
at Seething airfield Norfolk
1966

The Cosmic Wind was a fantastic aircraft to fly although very unforgiving. With only a 100hp RR Continental engine the author had 360mph indicated as he opened the Sywell Airshow in 1965.

The British Team for The World Aerobatic Competition at Moscow in 1966. Left to right; Neil Williams - died ferrying a Heinkel He111 from Spain. The author, Taff Taylor, a very old fighter pilot - the MoD banned him from going to Moscow as he was an ex-U-2 Spyplane pilot. Barry Tempest was dropped from team and Robin D'Erlanger.

The authors Harvard IV. His sons Alexander and Edward each logged over 100 hours on the type. The taller boy on the right is a Godson, Ben Coghlan.

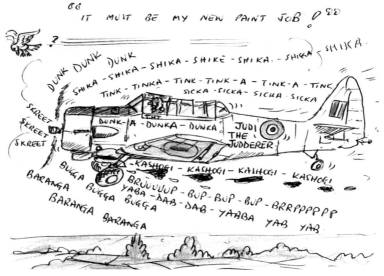

Eddie Edwards engineer, cartoonist and artist was horrified by the engineering state of my Harvard as evidenced by his Xmas card.

de Havilland collection flypast. The author acquired all seven Moths in the late sixties and early seventies. The Moth Minor cost £400 and the Tiger Moth £500.

de Havilland DH.83 Fox Moth G-ACEJ at Old Warden in the 1980s. The intriguing Fox Moth. Four passengers were carried in the cabin while the pilot braved the elements. This aircraft was destroyed in a fireball at Old Warden when a Beechcraft crashed into it killing three out of the four occupants.

The author owned this Grumman Avenger for nineteen years and flew it for 300 hours. The commentator at Biggin Hill Air Fair wondered aloud whether the pilot was fatter than the aircraft. Only John Blake could say that and live.

Getting airborne and landing the Avro Triplane is child's play. Manoeuvring it without ailerons certainly is not.

An original German First World War LVG C.VI and a beast to fly. The aircraft was owned by the Mod/RAF who gave it to the IWM. The IWM do not fly their aircraft so it was grounded and sent to Cosford.

The author was 'a Collection' pilot for 29 years. Here he is flying two of the nicer handling aircraft. (above) The beautiful Hawker Hind and (below) the SE5A fighter from the First World War. History in one's hands.

Alex Henshaw's old Hawker Tomtit. Here flown by the author after his accident at the Mildenhall Airshow. The undercarriage went into a trench during the landing roll in front of the VIP enclosure and television cameras.

The author flying the viceless Avro Tutor at Old Warden.

The author about to fly the Shuttleworth Trust's Avro Triplane. The gloves are worn to hide white knuckles from showing on photographs.

John Gerstorfer's beautiful ex-RCAF Silverstar. The author flew this aircraft on its last flight from Duxford to North Weald in 1999.

The author getting in some unlicensed float time in Tom Storey's Cub.

The author flying his Avenger in close formation on the Duxford B-17 Sally-B for George Bush Senior on 27th September 2002.

Newly wed in 1968. The Stately Home has its own lake and aerodrome. The author is downwind in his de Havilland Moth Minor with photo by the new 'love of my life' but this one also became the mother of my children..

The author was lucky enough to fly all the aircraft in this well known photograph. From left to right Hurricane, first flown in 1996, Spitfire in 1971, Meteor in 1958, Hunter in 1958, Javelin in 1961 and the Lightning in 1967.

'Going Home'. The author returning to Horsey Island after a day instructing on Jet Provosts.

Wg Cdr Bower, the Wing Commander Flying (and my old friend from the Equator Club in Nairobi) standing by the ground crews' quarters. He was very affable and friendly and we had a nice chat until he said "Have you managed to avoid being Orderly Officer since Rhodesia, Tony?" I replied in the affirmative and he said "Well, your luck has just run out. Three days starting next Monday", turned on his heel and left. A week later a Beverley flew into a hill at night thirty miles north of Khormaksar killing all on board and when the dust had settled, Wg Cdr Bower was ordered home. He very kindly invited John Volkers and myself to, as he called it, 'A farewell dinner for the bad boys'. I felt sorry for him but three dead Hunter pilots, a Beverley crew and our unauthorised low flying, all within six months was too much for the HQ staff and a scapegoat was needed.

Suddenly the boss wanted to see me. It had come to my notice that this was seldom to say "Well done on the range last week HT" or to compliment me on some job or other; it always presaged trouble. Come to think of it, life had been much the same at school. This time there was trouble up-country and as I had had several trips on convoy duty as Forward Air Controller, and had had more other up-country experience than the large number of new pilots, he had decided to send me. This trip was different from the others; two tribes had been fighting over a water hole in the North East corner of the protectorate, quite close, in fact, to Oman. I was to be given a Land Rover and two guards from the Aden Protectorate Levies and dropped at a desert strip adjacent to Bir Thamud. There would be a lorry there with more APL troops in it who would drive with us to rendezvous before dawn the following day with a Foreign Office Arabist, Julian Johnson, formerly with the Kings Shropshire Light Infantry. The lorry set off with my radio-equipped Land Rover following. We did not follow any track but drove, initially, over hard flat desert, and then along dried up water courses (wadis) making very slow progress. Then the lorry broke down and I was able to see, first hand, one of the worlds' engineering marvels, the ability of Arab drivers to mend their vehicles by day or night with very few tools. Our problems ranged from punctures to trouble in the gearbox but, eventually, very late at night, we covered the forty odd miles and found Julian Johnson. JJ was trying to settle an argument between two very warlike tribes as to who should own the waterhole, his plan was that they would each approach him from either side of the wadi and he would conduct peace talks. My job was to arrange for a firepower demonstration by a Shackleton of 37 Squadron. Signals were sent to Aden, the tribes advanced on each other from either side with JJ, myself and our little party in the middle as the jam in the sandwich. As the tribes drew nearer bullets whistled overhead; "Just fraternal greetings" said JJ and then they settled down to negotiations. At around two o'clock, to my amazement, a Shackleton came into view. A big four-engined development of the Lancaster, 'the Shack' had nose mounted 20mm cannon and I was very pleased to see it, not having been very sure that the Lat and Long position I had given was accurate. Negotiations were halted while the top of a small adjacent hill was turned to dust, impressing everyone; in the still air the cannon sounds magnificent except, I should imagine, when aimed at you. After the firepower demo I was supposed to drive home, but JJ took delivery of an Arab who had stopped a bullet in the arm and was obviously very ill. When he took off the dressings the arm fell off as it had turned gangrenous. I sent a personal signal to the SASO asking for a Scottish Aviation Twin Pioneer to be sent, to save the man's life, and was amazed to get a confirming signal for an early arrival the next day. I found a more or less level patch and spent an hour removing stones and then waited. Suddenly I heard engines in the distance and could just see the aircraft orbiting the wrong place some way off. Finally, at the nearest point on their orbit, I just got them to hear my radio transmission and gave them a visual homing; they landed and took the very sick man to Mukalla where he received proper treatment, recovered, and walked back to his tribe a distance of several hundred miles. Very tough people.

I spent another night with JJ and set off at dawn to drive some three hundred miles west from Bir Thamud to the Wadi Hadramaut and thence another hundred miles to Mukulla. In my trusty Land Rover, accompanied by my more or less trusty pair of APL soldiers I set off westwards to gain access to the Hadramaut valley. We got bogged down in sand dunes; our wireless set failed; we drank our normal water supply and then the emergency one from a previously petrol filled jerry can and then we had none left. When we finally arrived at the entrance to the legendary Wadi we were very, very thirsty, my lips had swollen and blackened and we needed water badly. Suddenly we came on a little irrigation channel. I stopped our trusty Rover, leaped out and plunged my face into the little running stream, my Arab companions doing likewise. When I had finished I noticed a camel fifty yards or so upstream of me cooling its private parts in the water from which I had drunk. There were no ill effects. We drove through the towns of Shibam, Sayun, and Tarim with their amazing architecture and rich merchants' houses built from wealth generated in the East Indies over the centuries. We refuelled, re-watered and rested at a small government-owned house in Shibam and then, on the fourth day of our journey, set off for Mukulla through hills up to 7000'. Nearing Mukulla we rounded a bend and saw a wonderful sight. There was a Land Rover, a table with a white cloth on it laid for tea, with the tea in a teapot. An Englishman from the Foreign & Colonial Service sat in a chair at the table with two servants standing behind him; it was tea-time and I had truly seen the last days of the Raj. After such a journey memories remain, surprisingly all very favourable. The beauty of the edge of the great Empty Quarter of Arabia with its very heavy dews at night; the silence of the desert at dawn; the thick mists, a few feet deep, until the merciless sun consumes them; the singing sand dunes which in the heat of the day leave one's ears ringing, and yet, from no discernible noise source. Most of all I remember our encounter, on a flat piece of desert, with an Arab who slowly emerged from the shimmering heat haze in the middle of nowhere just walking. He carried a goatskin water bottle and a big Dhab lizard that he had killed, and nothing else. He had a minimum of a hundred miles to go to Bir Thamud where at least there was water - of a sort. Amazing people. Eventually at the end of day five we drove into Mukulla and the next day I flew back to Aden in a DC-3. My previously new Land Rover was scrapped.

Government House was the apex of social life in the anthill that was the Aden colony; at least it was from the perspective of a very junior ant. At government house Volkers had been friends with HE's daughter while I had to make do with the ADC, Phillip Boys-Stones, an engagingly eccentric Flight Lieutenant in a very non-flying appointment. Phillip had brought an Arab dhow, enjoyed sailing it in Aden harbour and, at a party one evening, invited me to go sailing with him the next day. I turned up at Government House at the appointed hour and was warmly greeted; we had a cup of tea and a chat until the conversation turned to his newly acquired dhow. I listened attentively until he said that he had to go to play tennis with HE's daughter but, as I was so obviously keen on sailing, perhaps I would like to have a sail with him next week in his Arab dhow. I said that I would love to but I never did go out in it.

Back on the Squadron, Volkers was suffering from a severe lack of female company and unless I was mistaken, I was convinced I had similar symptoms, so a return visit to Rhodesia was planned, as it seemed a shame to leave such talent with nothing but a few Neanderthal colonial males for company. Travel in those days was not easy; we hitched an airlift to Mombasa with the RAF, flew to Zanzibar and thence to Salisbury. The girls were terrific and on the third day announced that they had had a competition and that the score was 13 – 12; I could not make out what they were talking about. When it was all over John and I were helped up the steps onto a Vickers Viscount and the girls stood on the airport apron and waved us goodbye. We never saw them again.

In Mombasa we had to wait two days for our transport back to Aden. John lay on his bed smoking a Balkan Sobranie 'black Russian' cigarette – his favourite brand, he would smoke no other – when, in a philosophical moment, he suddenly said that he wanted to live life to the full as he did not expect ever to see his twenty-third birthday. He didn't. After a major emergency in his Hunter he ejected, as it exploded, and he was caught in the fireball. It was a very sad loss for both me and the Royal Air Force. Years later I called on his parents in Malta where his father had retired from the Army as a Brigadier. Afterwards I wished I had not done so as it made them sad.

My time on 8 Squadron was coming to an end but the Wadi Hadramaut still gripped me. Mike Seymour who had been a friend on 63 Squadron had arrived and I led him on a sector reconnaissance to see this unknown gem. Fitted with 2 x 230 and 2 x 100 gallon underwing tanks, our Hunters had 'long legs' and could easily do a High, Low, High, sortie. It was a beautiful day and we descended to Tarim, the eastern-most town, reduced speed to 250 knots, which is very slow for a Hunter, and drifted down the 100 miles at 1000' just wondering at the fertility and the architecture. We flew back to Aden to find the boss in a state as after two hours he thought we must have crashed, not knowing that our time at 250 knots had given us a much longer sortie than normal. It was not my last sighting of the great Wadi, childhood home of Osama bin Laden, as our Squadron Engineering

Officer, Mike Murden, and I borrowed a Meteor which I flew to the gravel strip at Mukulla whence we DC-3'd into Sayun, and for a few days, we explored the whole valley in a government Land Rover. In Tarim we were mistaken for 'Yahudi' (Jews) and ran for our vehicle in a welter of stones before finally escaping. I flew the Meteor back to Aden after four days.

And now the end of my two-year tour was nigh. In my last few days on the Squadron I did lots of flying. One day I flew three range sorties, all with both guns and RP. When I had finished I put a total of one hour in my logbook and I was completely exhausted. On one of the sorties I got 68% on the air-to-ground targets and 4 yards average error with my rockets and as I could now navigate as well it seemed a pity to go home when my training was finally complete. But I did, in a Bristol Britannia, to an amazingly green England.

Chapter 14

HOME AGAIN

I arrived on April 14th 1961, to a wet and windy night at RAF Lyneham and almost longed for the heat and dust of Arabia. I also wondered what the future held in store for me. First things first, however, and one of my secret longings was due to be fulfilled – a little bit of flying with the Royal Navy in a Hawker Sea Hawk. In those days pilots returning from overseas had to report personally to the Air Ministry (known colloquially as 'the Air Box') for their new posting and my appointment was not until the end of April. In addition, one was entitled to a free rail ticket to anywhere within the United Kingdom, and so it seemed to make good financial sense to optimise this benefit and get my rail pass to Elgin, near Inverness in Scotland, where the RN operated a Sea Hawk conversion unit with the grand title of 'No.738 Squadron Royal Naval Operational Fighter School' at RNAS Lossiemouth. The train journey took forever but finally I arrived in the evening of 17th April. I hoped that the Commander Air had received my letter taking him up on his offer, made in the 8 Squadron crew room over a year previously, to the effect that if I got myself to Lossiemouth he would let me fly the Sea Hawk. I had written a reminder to him from Aden, but had not actually received a reply by the time I had left, so I was travelling in hope.

On the morning of April 18th I reported to the Commander Air, Cdr. Noble, who had had my letter and was quite happy to let me fly one of his Sea Hawks; better still he promised me four trips and sent for Lieutenant Simon Creasy to conduct my conversion flying. I had known Simon briefly at Valley before going to Chivenor and he came over to the Commander Air's office and took me off to 738 Squadron. Conversion to a new type in the RAF involved lectures and exams but the RN seemed a little more relaxed; Simon gave me a cup of coffee, a set of Pilots Notes and said that he would be back in an hour. He was, and after being given a chance to ask the usual questions I was kitted, up ready for a mid-day take off.

The Sea Hawk was, to my eye, a very pretty aircraft powered by a 5000lb thrust Rolls Royce Nene. I had only ever seen one before and that was at

Waterbeach when Lt. Paul Perks had flown in for lunch with his old friends on 63 Squadron. I never met him but watched from afar and, while he was reminiscing with his contemporaries, I slipped out to his aircraft and climbed into 'the office'. It had that Hunter feel about it, with even better visibility, but more like a single-seat Vampire, as it was much closer to the ground. Best of all it had folding wings, which, I now knew, were operated by one little switch on the port console.

Simon Creasy showed me the external checks, helped me strap to in and made sure that I knew all the taps, levers and switches. Once happy that I knew all that was needed, we went through the pre start drills and then, magical moment, I pressed the button to fire the starter cartridge. I was quite familiar with the noise and the smoke from my Venom days and, once everything was running, I unfolded the wings. Simon supervised my take-off checks and then waved goodbye as I called for 'taxi'. It is not often that one feels at home in an aircraft while taxiing out for a first solo, but I certainly did in the Sea Hawk. My only disappointment came on take-off when I could not believe how slowly it accelerated; my last two trips on 8 Squadron had been a fortnight earlier, one in a Meteor T.7 and the other a Hunter FGA.9, and the big reduction in thrust that came with the Sea Hawk surprised me when it should not have done. I was allowed four trips and four trips I flew. The first was the usual general handling with plenty of aerobatics and three circuits, but the last three were much more practical, including 'non-live' air to ground and RP on the range and one session using MADLS, the Mirror Assisted Deck Landing System, used by the RN for carrier landings. The practice MADLS unit was on the ground at Lossiemouth and not bouncing about on the ocean, but it did seem very simple to use, at least when it was glued down.

My view of the Sea Hawk was that it was a lovely handling aircraft, excellent for any low-level ground attack work, but I cannot believe that it would ever have out-fought a MIG-15 in any air combat situation, even when new. The Nene engine in the Sea Hawk flew with the USAF in the F-80 and, thanks to Comrade Attlee the then UK prime minister, being overcome with fraternal socialist feelings, the MIG-15 as well. It was a great tribute to Stanley Hooker at Rolls Royce that the same engine should power aircraft from the three world military powers of that era.

I called on Commander Noble, thanked him for his kindness, and had my logbook signed up with another new type. I was 23. I had 865 hours total flying and was qualified on Jet Provost, Vampire, Meteor, Hunter, Venom and Sea Hawk, not forgetting the Chipmunk. I did not wish to know about my 100 hours as a second pilot on Hastings. I had no idea what my next posting was to be but I had to catch a train to London to find out in a personal interview at the Air Ministry.

Travelling overnight from Scotland was the 1960s equivalent of the Red eye flight from New York in the eighties. In those days I was a member of the Royal Aero Club, at 119 Piccadilly, so after a decent breakfast, and suitably dressed in my smartest suit, I set off for the Air Ministry in Theobalds Road, High Holborn. I thought I would ask for a Hunter posting, with Javelins as my second choice and, if all else failed, an instructor's course. Things were not quite that simple. At the appointed hour I was summoned into the presence of a Wing Commander but even before I had sat down I was getting bad vibrations. He had my 1369 confidential report on officers and was studying it; then he studied it again.

"This is the worst report I have ever seen on any officer", he started, "Do you realise you have four 'starred' items?" In fact I did not know, even though 'starred' items were supposed to be drawn to the attention of the miscreants. My 8 Squadron boss, who had never had a bad word to say to me, even though he should have done, had well and truly fixed me. The Wing Commander looked up. "I can tell you one thing for certain. You will never fly another RAF aeroplane while you remain in the Service". I can remember a surge of indignant rage as I replied "In that case, Sir, I must resign my commission". Things were not looking good. "You won't, and you will go where you are sent. I am posting you to Air Traffic Control". Dear God, not that. "I am quite prepared to be a flying instructor if there is nothing else" I countered; unwisely it seemed, as it elicited a very firm "You are the last sort of person we want as a flying instructor". I had nothing left. "I must insist that I be allowed to resign my commission, Sir; if I am not suitable to serve on a Squadron, then I cannot be suitable in Air Traffic or anywhere else". I was told to go outside and wait. I waited, and waited. A man came down the corridor. "You look miserable," he said, "what is the matter?" I had not realised that I was showing any emotion but I poured out my story. I had been 'busted' for low flying, lost six months seniority and then been an exemplary Squadron member with 'above average' assessments for weapons work for the last ten months. My CO had not said anything bad but, presumably on the basis of the low flying episode, I had had four starred items; 'discipline zero', 'example to subordinates zero', etc., and now some illegitimately conceived Wing Commander was proposing that I become an Air Traffic Controller so, naturally enough, I had resigned my commission. I was very grateful for the patience and kindness shown in listening to my tale of woe by this most civil civil servant. It turned out to be a very lucky break.

After half an hour or so my 'friendly' Wing Commander summoned me back to his office. He still had my 1369. "I gather you have already met Air Commodore Strong, our head of department, and he thinks you would make a good ADC – but you won't be able to fly in that job". I gulped. Air Marshals had not given me much happiness so far in my life – how on earth could I be an ADC? "Will it be in Fighter Command?" I asked. "Yes, I am sending you for interview with the Air Officer Commanding No.11 Group, at RAF Ouston in Northumberland. He will see you in two days time, but I must tell you he will know all about this dreadful report." And with that I was shown the door. I was beginning to feel that perhaps I would not make 'Air' rank if I stayed in the Royal Air Force.

I rang Air Vice Marshal Maguire's ADC, Mike White, and made an appointment for the interview, following which panic set in. I did not have a No.1 Service Dress Uniform. It had been lost while in store at my tailors. I had a brain wave! Messrs Moss Bros of Covent Garden could hire anything, so I went straight there and sure enough an extremely smart Service Dress Uniform No.1, RAF officers for the use of, was available and, with minor alterations, would be ready in time. "I must have Pilots Wings," I said to the assistant. "Certainly Sir. Some film work is it?" "Not exactly," I replied. The next day I caught the train to Newcastle. I have always enjoyed travelling by train but for me the run north through all those magic Selby, York, Doncaster names, redolent with British Industrial history, have a very special ring to them. At Newcastle, I was met by a driver from Ouston, who took me back to the mess ready for my interview the next day with the Air Marshal. Naturally, as a top fighter pilot I wasn't in the least bit nervous at the thought; well, only a little bit!

The buzzer in Mike White's office sounded. He stood up and went through to the AOC's office, returning a moment later with a terse "You're on". "Flying Officer Haig-Thomas" he announced as I entered the holy of holies. The Air Marshal smiled and invited me to take a seat; he seemed a nice man and almost human. I noticed with that sinking feeling that he was reading my dreaded 1369 – eventually he put it down. A normal sort of interview followed. After a few minutes he said that I should not be too concerned about the low flying episode, as he too had suffered an identical fate for the same offence when he had been a young flying officer, and it did not seem to have harmed his career. It was lunchtime and the AOC asked me if I would like to join him in the mess for lunch; as we walked the short way to the officers mess a Meteor 'broke' into the circuit for landing. I followed its path round the circuit and the AOC noting my interest in it said "Are you Meteor qualified Tony?", I replied that I was, was current and had an instrument rating. "Excellent" said the Air Marshal, "Mike White isn't so we can save a huge amount of time visiting our remoter stations like Chivenor in Devon and Stornoway in the Hebrides. I hate sitting in the back of an Anson." Things were looking good, it seems that I would get the job and fly officially; a dangerous longing to ring the illegitimate Wing Commander with the news was suppressed and after lunch I was appointed ADC to the AOC No.11 Group Fighter Command – in waiting: or, to put it another way, assistant to the assistant to the Air Marshal.

Back to London to return my very smart Moss Bross uniform and spend a couple of nights in town in search of some fairly urgently needed female company. I booked into the Royal Aero Club and immediately bumped into Peter Martin, a fellow Hunter pilot who had been ADC to the legendary C-in-C Bomber Command, 'Bing' Cross. I asked for his advice and hints on how to be a good ADC."Oh, that is easy – just carry a box of matches," the sage replied. "But I don't smoke'" I said. "Then definitely carry a box of matches," I was told. It was good advice from which I had an early dividend.

With my leave over, and wearing a smart new uniform I took up my new job. It was 15th May 1961. I was twenty-three and a half and a little apprehensive about my new appointment in case a catastrophe developed from a piece of Haig-Thomas maladministration. Knowing myself better than anyone else, I knew this was almost inevitable. My predecessor still had four months of his tour to do so I was to attend a Junior Command and Staff School course at Bircham Newton in Norfolk. This course was designed for up and coming young officers before they went to Staff College. In those days it was in fact the first term of a Staff College Course, but best of all Bircham Newton was very close to the Central Fighter Establishment at West Raynham where, hopefully, I should get some flying.

Meanwhile back at Ouston I had to go through the dreadful RAF 'arrivals' procedure, which involved visiting every section of the Station and obtaining a signature from the NCO in charge. Soon I was footsore and weary and very close to the hangars. Time to introduce myself to the HQ Communications flight! There seemed to be plenty of pilots and aeroplanes but no flying – a situation that I managed to remedy with a check flight in a Chipmunk and a full asymmetric and instrument check in the Meteor. The next day I flew the Meteor to Middleton St George to collect a Staff Officer and then the day after, the 17th May 1961, I flew four Meteor sorties including a trip to St Mawgan in Cornwall completing seven hours in my first three days in a ground job. I hoped that the illegitimate Wing Commander was eating his heart out.

I then spent three weeks with Mike White learning the ropes and getting to know the names of various staff officers, many of whom had had wonderful careers in WWII. The senior Air Staff Officer was Air Commodore 'Micky' Mount who had the office opposite mine each with our own door to the AOC. MM had been a very successful Spitfire pilot in the Battle of Britain and wore a DSO and DFC under his wings. He had been educated at Eton and Oxford where he had read law and learned to fly with the Oxford University Air Squadron; he also had a very characteristic stammer and was a delightful - and, to me - helpful man in every way. We shared the same educational background and, while his father had been killed in the First World War, mine had died in Normandy during the second. Along the corridor I found another office 'Group Captain J.B. Tait DSO DFC' Senior Admin Officer it said on the door. I knocked and went in to introduce myself. Now I am not really into medals but I had never seen a man with three DSOs and two DFCs. One just had to be impressed. 'Willie' Tait had led 617 Dambusters Squadron in the attack on the Tirpitz in the Norwegian Fjords among many other gallant deeds and now here he was in charge of Group Admin. However there was not one single file or piece of paper on his desk and he was obviously very bored, with his eyes half closed. One had to admire his ability to delegate. Further down the corridor a door proclaimed Group Captain McCarthy with various academic qualifications. A big, jovial, untidy man 'Doc' McCarthy was the Group Medical Officer and both he and the AOC had been prisoners of war in Japan and both had an unrepressed hatred of anything Japanese. McCarthy had had an interesting experience in Nagasaki. He had been assigned to unloading a ship in the harbour when an air raid alarm enabled him to hide behind a big concrete block for an unauthorised smoke. As he struck a match for a light-up there was a solar event when the Nagasaki atom bomb detonated within a mile of him. He was saved from a heat blast or radiation death by being in the best possible place, through pure luck, behind the big block of concrete several feet thick, a rare example of smoking saving life.

Going down the ranks my next call was to Wing Commander John Rogers. He had a namesake who became an Air Marshal, but this version of JR and I took an immediate dislike to each other which was unfortunate because his empire included the Operational Conversion Units at Chivenor for Day Fighter pilots, and most important of all, 228 OCU at Leeming, home of the mighty Javelin All Weather Fighter, sometimes known as the Gloster Dragmaster. I had always kept an eye open for new types to fly and to be on the HQ staff of the Javelin OCU was a signpost to heaven. The right time for me to go on a Short Course would be when the AOC was on leave but now was not the right time to ask. I would have to launch a sustained charm offensive on this rather un-charming (to me) man; I am sure his wife liked him but in retrospect perhaps there was trouble on the home front which gave him his difficult approach to life.

A few days later, and after some grovelling sycophancy, he seemed to be less antagonistic and I thought the time was right to try and wangle a Javelin conversion. The AOC was on leave during the last week in July and my JC & SS course at Bircham Newton finished on the 20th; perfect timing for a Javelin five-day short course. I knocked on the Wing Commander's door and entered; coming straight to the point I broached the subject. "Certainly not," he said, "the Air Force has no need for you to fly the Javelin and you must learn that the RAF is not a flying club." This was a bit of a set-back but on my by now proven-principle that God helps those who help themselves I returned to my desk in Mike White's office and wrote to Wing Commander W.E.T. Thomas, who I had never met and who was the Wing Commander Flying, at Leeming. I headed my letter from Fg. Off. A Haig-Thomas ADC to AOC 11 Group, and asked if I could join the short course on the Javelin starting on the 26th July. Two days later I had a phone call to say that I would need to do the three-week ground school course before flying the Javelin. He didn't say I couldn't fly it so I asked whether, if I could pass the ground school exam without the course, would that do? "Certainly," he said, "but you must get at least 95%." I promised I would and avoided Wing Commander. Rogers until I left for Bircham Newton.

Chapter 15

STAFF COLLEGE AND A JAVELIN

The Junior Command and Staff School was originally the first term of a Staff College Course; it was designed to prepare junior officers for staff appointments and then, when they were senior officers, for a full-bloodied Staff College course which would be the make or break of their careers. Students were taught how to write reports, analyse simple administrative problems, the elements of Air Force Law and legal procedures and, most usefully, public speaking. It was, in retrospect, a wonderful experience, and the report writing and public speaking, in particular, has been really useful throughout my life. The Course was run from the beautiful tranquil setting of Bircham Newton a few miles west of Fakenham in Norfolk; it was a large grass field with huge 1930 hangars that during the war was the base from which RN Swordfish had mined the Kiel Canal. The Officers Mess was one of the best in the country, with a magic mess manager and cuisine that was far too good for anyone predisposed to weight gain. The main attraction for me, however, was the location, only a mere ten miles to the south east lay the Central Fighter Establishment from where the really great pilots of Fighter Command, minus myself of course, flew Hunters, Meteors, Canberras and, best of all, Javelins. The JC & SS Course allowed Wednesday afternoons off for sports but virtually none of the students on my course played any; they stayed in their rooms and wrote up their essays and analyses. For me Wednesday afternoons were the gateway to yet another heaven and on the first Wednesday I skipped lunch and headed for the CFE at West Raynham.

One needs luck in life and even in the Royal Air Force of the fifties and sixties one could not just walk in and demand an aircraft to fly, but I found the instrument training flight run by Stan Sollitt, my old Flight Commander from my Vampire days, and in no time at all I was airborne for a check flight in a Meteor followed by a short solo. I convinced myself that keeping current in an unarmed Meteor was essential if the Red hoards, who were probably massing behind the iron curtain even as I flew, were to be deterred from a full frontal attack. There was a further dividend to come. Stan Sollitt had a Javelin T.3, the trainer version, on his unit and he lent me a set of Javelin Pilots' Notes and a copy of the Javelin ground exam. Best of all, he promised me a T.3 ride before I went to try the beast for real.

Back at Bircham Newton reality began to set in; the Javelin was a very complex piece of engineering.To fly it required a three-week full-time course whereas the Canberra, for example, also a twinjet of similar size and weight but a bomber, required only a week's study. The real problem however was that the JC & SS course that I was on also required a very high workload - which was why my fellow students caught up with their studies on Wednesdays instead of going flying. Copious amounts of official writing and studying were required in the evenings and at weekends – fine and no trouble, unless you were trying to work for a Javelin technical exam at the same time. It was summer and my two months were up; on my Wednesday afternoons I had flown seven Meteor trips, three hours in Chipmunks flying cadets, and Stan came good with a back-seat ride in the Javelin T.3. My Administrator's Course was over and it was time for an interview with my course leader Wing Commander Smith-Carrington. The expression on his face was not reassuring. "I am afraid we cannot pass you Haig-Thomas. We have assessed you as quite unsuitable for Staff Work. Where are you posted to?" "HQ, 11 Group, Sir, as ADC." "I see. Well I wish you luck when your report arrives on the AOC's desk." The interview was over and I couldn't argue with his view as I also regarded myself as totally unfit for any ground appointment; neither could I tell him that I had worked really hard for the last two months - but not too much on admin procedures. I couldn't tell him either that I knew more about the Javelin than most squadron pilots flying them, and it wouldn't have interested him if I had as his flying days were long gone. Finally, since he was an old Harrovian I could hardly expect any sympathy for an Old Etonian! No time for recriminations though. I had to pack and get to Yorkshire, to RAF Leeming. My ground exam was the next day followed by my promised Javelin flying, about which I hoped Wing Commander Rogers had not yet found out.

RAF Leeming is in Yorkshire and lies beside the A1 road south of Catterick and north of Boroughbridge. Ever since I had been in the Royal Air Force it had been the home of the Night Fighter Conversion Unit, taking first tour pilots from Day Fighter Squadrons, converting them on to the Javelin and then teaching them how to creep up behind a target at night or in cloud – or both. The unit's designation and title was No.228 Javelin Conversion Unit. I didn't like the sound of the operational role - boring for any ground attack pilot - but Glosters big double delta appealed to every pilot instinct I possessed. It was huge compared to the day fighters I had flown up to that time; twice the weight and three times the volume, at a guess; and was already hopelessly out of date by the time it entered service in the mid fifties - certainly so when compared with its peers the Phantom and Starfighter. In fact, by the early sixties the RAF and Iceland were the only NATO countries not to have aircraft with level sonic capability. Tactical capabilities of the Javelin did not really concern me; I was only interested in it as a flying machine, not its operational role. It did in the fifties what the Mosquito and Meteor NF series had done before; the radar was a little better but it was much faster and heavier and the big Delta wing appealed to the Walter Mitty in me.

I sat the ground school examination on Monday morning and scored 97% on the 100 questions, helped, I must admit, by the copy of the examination paper given to me by Stan Sollitt. It had not helped that much however because to answer all the questions correctly required a total knowledge of the aircraft, its systems, limitations and procedures. One question - 'List in detail the take-off checks' - required one sheet of A4 by itself. I finished the exam, had lunch and reported to the Flight Simulators where I was put through the usual chain of sequential, progressive, nightmarish and unlikely emergencies until five o'clock when, totally exhausted, I retired to the mess for dinner and an extremely early night. Tomorrow would be for real.

One of the great things about jet aircraft is that although they are complex in engineering terms, they are all extremely easy to fly; that is, to take off, fly around and land. Unlike their predecessors they require very little stick and rudder skills in the landing pattern. The use of the aircraft as a weapon is another matter. A night intercept in a single-seat radar-equipped aircraft, like a Lightning for example, while flying single handed and peering into a radar scope, requires a huge set of very demanding skills, far removed from the piston era of Douglas Bader, and much more in line with the computer game skills of a contemporary twelve year old. I didn't need the difficult bit, only the fun of flying but in any case the Javelin had a man in the back to do all the hard work.

On the 27th July I met my instructor Flt. Lt. Ginger I was pleased it wasn't the legendary Pole Flt. Lt 'Andy' Andrewsjki, whose warped sense of humour had manifested itself when, after landing with one of his students, the conversation went as follows: "Now then Smith, what is your name?'" "Well, it is Smith, Sir." "No, no, Smith, I know that. What does your mother call you?" "John, Sir." "Right John, you are scrubbed." I have not attempted to mimic the very strong Polish accent but it did show that he had a human side after all – well, sort of. Flt Lt. Ginger and I walked to the aircraft. It seemed huge – perhaps I couldn't fly something this big after all. After the usual walk-round checks I climbed the ladder and settled in to the cockpit which was also huge but, thanks to months of study and my simulator time, everything was reassuringly familiar. I completed my detailed left-to-right checks and then was ready to start; at the back of the cockpit on the right hand console were two black, spring loaded, flaps each covering an unnecessarily large red button. I pressed one – somewhere a long way behind me, there was a deep explosion; all the engine instruments started to come alive and then there was a deep resonant boom in the intakes as the various harmonic frequencies coincided to produce a very distinctive noise that was common on all night fighter stations in the fifties. I loved it.

With the second engine running we taxied out. I ran through the take-off checks as normal, on the move, and thence to the runway. The flight itself was a bit of an anticlimax – the aircraft had natural four-axis stability which made it very easy to fly especially in the landing and approach phase – most useful on a dirty night when short of fuel. One feature of the Javelin which was really impressive was the deceleration from 400 knots; when the airbrakes were applied it produced a linear G force of over one at the start. Flt. Lt. Ginger was pleased. We did a second trip and flew supersonic, actually with less effort than the Hunter, and then recovered with a radar talk-down and some single engine flying and circuits. Flt. Lt Ginger was still pleased. I flew the T.3 solo the next day and then a further five trips in the FAW.5 (Fighter All Weather Mk 5); I had my logbook signed up as a qualified-on-type, Javelin pilot, and drove north to Northumberland, to RAF Ouston, to start life as an ADC. Within three months of being told I would never fly again, I had checked out in the Sea Hawk and Javelin and had flown several hours in the Meteor, not to mention a few sorties in the humble Chipmunk. There was life after death after all.

I have tried to write this account of my life chronologically but as this section has been about the Javelin it seems appropriate to complete my saga of life with Glosters double delta because it had not quite ended. While acting as an ADC I was free when the AOC was away and freedom meant flying. The OC No.33 Squadron at RAF Middleton St George (now Teeside) was Wing Commander Caryl Gordon and they flew Javelin FAW.9 aircraft; it had much bigger engines with two enormous reheat nozzles at the back end and up to four Firestreak missiles. I had met Caryl on my first official visit with the AOC and he had offered me a chance to fly the Mk 9 if I could get a day off. On October 17th 1962 when the AOC was away I borrowed a Hunter from 92 Squadron at Leconfield, where the Group HQ was now based and flew to Middleton. A T.3 was waiting with an instructor who made me do all the pre-solo exercises and then I had a cockpit brief and supervised start in the Mk 9. For my first trip the back seat was occupied by an intrepid USAF Captain who could actually work the radar. We took off and at 1500' went straight into cloud. Then I had my eyes opened; as we climbed to 25000' a voice from the back suddenly started to tell me about all the other aircraft he could 'see' on his radar. "Left 11 o'clock, high, five miles," "Right 1 o'clock same height expedite climb." I was appalled. As a good single-seat pilot, when I climbed through cloud it had never occurred to me that there were any other aircraft anywhere near me. The Mk 9 had partial reheat that operated above 25,000' and I had looked forward to using it. "Standby for reheat," I said and moved the throttles forward. Nothing happened.Curses, I had forgotten the reheat master switches; rapidly switching them on I tried again. A dull thud followed and the reheat 'dolls-eyes' went black; the rate of climb increased, nothing else, it was very anti-climactic. I flew south east and called Leconfield (where 11 Group HQ had moved to) for a let-down and radar approach. I hoped the Javelin would be seen by lots of pilots on 19 and 92 Squadrons and they would wish that they too had a ground job. Alas no one ever noticed my low approach and go-around but it made me feel good. I flew back to

Middleton, landed, climbed into the 92 Squadron Hunter and flew home, arriving just before the airfield closed. I slept well that night.

Even this wasn't quite the end of the Javelin saga. Rather late in the day there strode into my office Wing Commander John Rogers; in his hand he held a piece of paper listing the names of all the successful graduates of the Javelin OCU at Leeming. He was very angry. "Gross disobedience.""Treating the RAF as a flying club," etc. etc. I tried to look humble and crestfallen and nothing more was ever said. God does help them who help themselves

Chapter 16

ADC TO THE AOC NO. 11(F) GROUP

I had no idea of the functions of an Aide de Camp, and only someone who has actually fulfilled that position will ever know anything about the role as, by and large, the functions of an ADC are hardly memoir stuff when compared with the distinguished military career of an Admiral, Air Marshal or General although he himself may well have served as an ADC whilst a young officer. The relationship between Senior Officer and ADC is vital; it is not master and servant but it nearly is, it is not father and son but that is close and, perversely, it is definitely not officer and subordinate but it is a mix of all three. The most important thing is that the two must genuinely like one another. Michael White, my predecessor, handed over two swords for use on formal visits, a set of golden aiguillettes with two hanging golden spikes worn round the left shoulder by the ADC, and round the right shoulder by the very Senior Officer. The spikes apparently were symbolic of pickets for the Senior Officer's horse but mercifully both the Air Marshals I was ADC to disliked horses as much as I did, and do. My day-to-day job involved opening the mail first thing in the morning and, when the boss arrived, taking it into him together with any papers that had been prepared by the HQ staff; the AOC would then list small jobs that he wished me to do and I would repair to my office to await a summons and get on with my tasks. I shared an office with a very pretty WAAF, SACW Cant, whose home was not far from mine in Essex; she caused me severe nervous problems because when I arrived in the morning she would be sitting demurely at her desk and, as surnames were the order of the day, I had to say "Good Morning Cant" – very carefully. Unlike my predecessor I could fly a Meteor and so I was the AOC's personal pilot as well when we were visiting various fighter stations within our parish; whilst carrying the Air Marshal we used the call sign 'Hadrian', being the power in the North, a practice now discontinued.

I was also in charge of 'the staff', comprising a driver, Corporal Malcolm Churchyard, (an unfortunate name as he came complete with a shiny black Jaguar saloon), and two indoor corporals, a cook and a butler - those were the days! 'The residence' was a beautiful Georgian House, The Grange. It was very large and, I felt, quite befitted an Air Marshal; it was however strangely bare without the acres of family portraits which should have lined the walls of such a fitting 'gents' res'. The AOC returned from leave and after a few days Mike White left for 92 Squadron to fly Hunters while I, with a great deal of trepidation, eased myself into my job.

No.11 Group had achieved huge fame in the Battle of Britain in the South but now our Group HQ was at RAF Ouston twenty miles west of Newcastle. The parish extended from Chivenor near Barnstaple in Devon, to Leconfield near Beverley in E. Yorkshire, to Leeming in N. Yorkshire, Middleton St George (now Teeside) west of Middlesbrough and finally Leuchars near St Andrews in Fife. These were our fighter bases, equipped with Hunters and Javelins. We had Radar Stations in Shetland, at Saxa Vord on the tip of the northernmost point and at Aird Uig on the North Atlantic coast thirty miles west of Stornoway; there were radar stations at Buchan near Banff, Boulmer in N. East Yorkshire and Patrington on the coast, east of Hull. These five radar heads overlapped to give a very good radar coverage which would have been excellent so long as the Russians came in at high level and were not unsporting enough to make a let-down and attack under the radar lobe at low altitude. Finally we had missile sites; these were Bloodhound air defence missiles with a range of around thirty miles. We 'owned' the missile test range at Aberporth on the Cardigan Bay coast line in Wales together with active missile sites deployed to protect Thor ICBM stations at Lindholme, Woodhall Spa, Dunholme Lodge, North Coates and one or two others; most of these were clustered west of Hull and, in my totally uninformed view, completely useless and manifestly very expensive. They were the source of my first ADC cock-up and it happened in my first week. The group intelligence officer used to wander round looking for, amongst other things, Russian spies. Soon after I had started he came into my office and asked for the file on the Missile Readiness states. These were delivered to my office every day for the AOC and, after he had seen them I had to lock them in a safe; they were marked SECRET in large letters. Keen to impress him I quickly opened the safe and, to my horror, found no file. When I suggested that the AOC must have it he said that he didn't as he himself had it! I had left it on my desk for a moment while I went down the corridor on some errand or other and he had chosen that time to come to see me, and found the file on my desk. He promised that no one else would know – this time. I hated the missile sites as I was bored when visiting them but amazed by the technology, and since we had to drive to them as they were not on air bases I was deprived of any flying. I was also horrified at the existence of the hapless personnel who had to man the control centres twenty-four hours a day in a dreadful little brick bunker. Many of their officers wore wings and must have joined the RAF to fly, much as I had done, and were now stuck in a no-hope job, going nowhere, with their youth slipping from them. Although not strictly in chronological sequence my affair with our missile bases has two other stories attached to it.

The AOC was particularly keen to see a missile launch and several times we arranged to go to Aberporth to see the sight; even I quite wanted to as well. There was however a snag in that every time a launch was scheduled a spy trawler from the Kremlin would sail into Cardigan Bay bristling with antennae to watch the launch, which then had to be cancelled, so the AOC never did see a Bloodhound launched and neither did I. The other time that Aberporth came into my life occurred one day when the AOC was away and Ben Hanson, the HQ Flight OC, rang me up and asked me to help him fly the Group Anson down to the Welsh Range. The weather was dreadful so Ben took off, set heading in the dear old nineteen thirties, twin engined, tail-dragger and then climbed out of the pilot's seat, leaving me to fly, as instructed by him from the back where the navigator's equipment was situated. Ben worked the radio associated with airways crossings and when we were a few miles from Aberporth came forward and took over for the landing. When we got home I entered four hours first pilot time in my logbook which seemed fair, as I had been the sole pilot, albeit not Captain; on top of that it was all on instruments and in cloud - but I had never taken off or landed. Sometime later I applied to the Civil Aviation Authority for a twin licence, citing my two hundred odd hours on Meteors only to be turned down as the Meteor was 'too heavy'. I then wrote again to say that I had four hours first pilot time on Ansons and was immediately granted a 'B' licence to allow me to fly any twin piston-engined aircraft of less than 12,500lbs. This was my first experience of weird civil bureaucratic thinking.

During my first week I flew the dreaded Wing Commander Rogers to

Leuchars, flew two solo aerobatic trips while he was busy, and then flew him back to Ouston saving him the flog up there in the Anson at 130 knots. In fact I flew five staff officers to various stations during my first month and took the AOC to a further five. One of these was to Chivenor where I scrounged a Hunter ride so that at the end of August, I had flown 27 hours during my first month in a ground job during which I was 'never to fly another RAF aircraft'. I once again, wished the illegitimate Wing Commander knew. It was amazing to me that so few of the group staff, most of whom wore wings, bothered to maintain Meteor currency but I certainly wasn't grumbling. My first real test of nerves came within ten days. It was the occasion of the group ball at Ouston and all the Air Ranking Officers from Fighter Command HQ as well as the AOC and SASO from No.12 Group were at a pre-ball reception at the Grange. I made sure that everyone's glass was full and while doing so I noticed my boss talking to the C-in-C Fighter Command who put a cigarette in his mouth and then patted his pockets for a light. Quick as a flash I appeared and lit his cigarette for him. "I didn't know you smoked, Tony," said the AOC. "I don't, Sir." "Very good" he said. I swelled with pride and silently thanked Peter Martin for his advice. Soon the AOC left for the ball and I was told to ease everyone out in twenty minutes and then I knew that cold hand of fear again. How could I, a rather undistinguished Flying Officer, get a dozen Air Ranking Officers to move? I started with the C-in-C, "I think we ought to be moving soon, Sir," he said "Certainly'" and did so, followed by all the others. I couldn't believe it. The C-in-C was Sir Hector MacGregor who, to my shame, I only discovered years later had a fantastic war record as a Hurricane pilot.

One day Squadron Leader 'Buck' Ryan, the staff officer responsible for day fighter operations at the Group HQ, was given a job that enabled me to see how to go about winning in life. It was at the weekly Group meeting; the AOC was in the chair and the subject of Air-to-Air gunnery came up and, specifically, the RAF's poor performance in the main NATO air weapons trophy, or AIRCENT, to give it its proper name. The AOC, in front of the meeting, told the Squadron Leader that he had five months, and any resources he needed, to ensure a victory for the RAF. 92 Squadron had lovely blue-painted Hunter F.6s and some very experienced second and third tour fighter pilots who had been posted in for the formation aerobatic team; those with the highest weapons assessments were the chosen few. They flew day after day on the Patrington range off the East Yorks coast. Then they went to Germany where they won – by miles. The AOC was pleased.

On another occasion, 'Buck' Ryan came into my office just as the AOC came into it from his door.Ryan explained to the AOC that 19 Squadron were detached to Skyrdstrup in Denmark but did not have the correct crystals for their radios and so could not cross-operate with the Danish Air Force. The crystals were all at Bovingdon but there was no staff officer with an instrument rating to fly them out. I could not believe my ears. Then the AOC turned to me and said, "Tony, you have one – why don't you do it?" I rushed down to the HQ Flight where Ben Hanson told me that the crystals and maps were ready for me at Bovingdon and that I was to stay in the aircraft during refuelling as it was late. An hour and a half after leaving my office I landed at Bovingdon where a navigator gave me some beautifully prepared maps and the crystals; perhaps navigators had their uses after all! Twenty minutes after landing at Bovingdon I was airborne again and heading for Jever in Germany. I had no navigation aids just one frequency, 117.9 - the RAF Common frequency, which, as it was in the middle of a NATO exercise, was filled with non-stop transmissions so I could not get Jever to answer my increasingly desperate calls. Eventually a voice said "Jever closed two months ago." At this time I had been airborne for over half an hour, all of it in cloud, at 30,000' in my un-pressurised cockpit and I knew I should never have trusted a navigator. I diverted to Wildenrath, landing just as the airfield was closing and very short of fuel, having had a most stressful flight which would have been so easy if I had had a local frequency for the airfield. The Wing Commander flying came down to see who had flown in and told me that I had been taxiing too fast – he was right, but I denied it. The next morning I arrived in Denmark, handed over the crystals and returned home. I had flown over nine hours in seven sorties during an elapsed twenty-four. September continued with a further eight sorties with the AOC to give me 25.45 hours for that month; I had never had so much flying or, on occasions, quite such demanding flying. Once we had planned a trip to Leuchars; it was a beautiful day but Leuchars was 'State Black'- no flying due to ice on the runway. The AOC asked if I was willing to fly - always a bad thing to ask me as I always said yes, well nearly always. We flew north and let down. I pulled the airbrakes out and burnt off fuel to an absolute minimum and then put the aircraft down as near to the runway threshold as I dared, shut down both engines, and raised the nose as high as I could to use aerodynamic braking. Leuchars had a very long runway and we rolled to a halt with a minimal use of brake on what looked like a non-icy patch. We were then towed in. In a flying appointment I would never have been authorised to make a flight like that.

The most demanding flights that I made with the AOC were to Stornoway in the Hebrides. In a nutshell I had no navigation aids, and there were no let down or radar approach aids available. All I could get was a true bearing from a man with a hand-operated homer and, as we approached the overhead position, he would announce that he was unable to give me a bearing. I then had to construct my own let-down, bearing in mind the lumps of rock hidden in the clouds all round Stornoway and the inevitable rain and low cloud that is endemic in the Western Isles. There was one final bit of excitement. If I started a let-down I had no diversion field so I was committed once I pulled back the throttles and deployed the airbrakes since an extra 100 gallons would be needed to fly the descent and then climb back to 30,000'. My fuel state would then be zero and I could go nowhere except down again. One of the main contributing factors to an accident is pressure. Now imagine my position; I have arrived in the near overhead to Stornoway, with the AOC in the back; on the ground waits the Aird Uig Station Commander. His station has been smartened up during the previous week, a huge lunch has been cooked, and everyone is awaiting the Air Marshal's arrival with the usual mix of excitement and nerves. Back in the cockpit I am feeling very uncomfortable; I have no formal limits, other than those I set myself, and in any accident I shall be solely to blame, and quite properly too, as it will have been my fault. My diversion field, and the only one at that, is Lossiemouth to which I can divert from the overhead leaving behind a very angry, anti-climaxed, Station CO and carrying a bored, cold Air Marshal faced with three and a half hours in an un-pressurised Meteor T.7, with virtually no heating, and an outside temperature of -50° to -60°C which was very close to the temperature inside. I made the trip four times in all and only diverted on one of them when I was given 1000' in light rain; in the Hebrides this can become 500' and zero visibility very quickly and death would have been probable for both of us.

My most memorable trip to Stornoway was one where the conditions on our arrival were actually the best I ever experienced – broken heavy cumulus at 2,500'. There was a jet-stream forecast with winds up to 200mph at 30,000' so at that height we could not make it; at 20,000' the winds were 100 mph but our fuel burn would have been too high but, at 37,000' we could make it even with a 100 mph head wind. I had the aircraft's ventral and pylon tanks filled, the AOC climbed aboard, together with some coffee and a sandwich for the journey overland to Aird Uig once we had landed. We set off, our track being the exact reciprocal of the Jet Stream (the technical name for these very high velocity high level winds). It became cold, then very cold; I touched a piece of metal on the hood with a bare finger and it flash froze onto the metal. We had cruise-climbed to 38,000' and after an hour I was starting to get niggles in my knee joints, a sure sign of the onset of 'the bends' but we were nearly there now. The temperature outside was -60° C. Suddenly a voice from the back said "I'm frozen Tony, I think I will have a cup of coffee." I thought nothing of it until there was a muffled roar from the back and a large part of the inside of the Meteor was covered with instantly flash frozen coffee. The boiling point of water depends on the ambient atmospheric pressure so the contents of the AOC's thermos turned to super-heated steam the moment he undid the top. Neither of us had even thought of that. After a successful let-down I taxiied in and shut down and, after we had climbed out, an amazing sight met our eyes. My left pylon tank had not fed and was filled with fuel at -60° so, as the warm moist Hebridean air flowed past it, the water vapour went from a gaseous state to solid ice instantaneously. After no more than five minutes the tank had doubled in size and was a huge, perfectly formed, aerodynamically shaped lump of ice.

The radar station at Saxa Vord is on Unst at the very northernmost tip of the Shetland Islands. When the sun shines it is very beautiful indeed, with a wondrous number and variety of sea birds. It is lashed by winds of immense force and has an uncomfortable amount of rain. In those days there was a small municipal airport at Sumburgh on the southern tip of the southernmost island big enough for an Anson but not a jet, so we always went by Anson. At Saxa Vord, depending on what was in season, we fished or shot snipe. The AOC told me that one day he and his wife and Mike White had left Sumburgh to refuel at Wick. The journey should have taken around 45 minutes so after an hour and a quarter he got up and went to the cockpit to see what has happening. The Master Pilot and Master Navigator were peering anxiously forward but told the AOC that it was just a little unforecast headwind. Ten minutes later the AOC went forward again and pointed out to them that they were steering 120° when they should have been on 220° and that they were flying right down the middle of the North Sea. When they finally reached Wick they were nearly out of fuel. Other excitements happened at Saxa Vord – this one was before my time and was recounted to me by my ADC predecessor, Mike White. There were some huts down on the shoreline at Saxa Vord where no one could go as they were 'top secret'; half a dozen engineers from the Bell telephone company worked there plus a U.S. Navy Lieutenant Commander and one of similar rank from the Royal Navy. I can vouch for this secrecy as the AOC was invited down to their huts during one of my visits. I wasn't allowed to go with him, and when the boss returned he told me that everything was covered up with sheets so that he couldn't see anything! The workers at the site had all their personal mail delivered to London and sent up to Saxa Vord as no-one was meant even to know that they were there. No one did, apparently, except the Russians. Shortly after 'the Huts' became operational a Russian submarine surfaced, dropped off a diver who cut some sections out of the cables that ran out under the sea, and then disappeared. It all happened so quickly that it was hardly noticed.Six months later an active Soviet spy ring was arrested at the Admiralty. Nothing was ever published so one suspects the hand of the 'D' Notice Committee, not so much to preserve a secret as to hide a shame. Now, of course, it is obvious that the cables were the UK end of the SOSUS submarine detection system, but in the early sixties the existence of SOSUS was unknown – unless you were in the Soviet GRU. 'Mac' Maguire liked fishing so we always took our rods and flies with us; in Shetland the fishing was free and in the summer there is virtually no darkness so one evening we thought we would try our luck – I was accompanied by a SNCO who watched me cast and cast without even a ripple showing; eventually he could stand it no longer. "Would you like to catch some fish, Sir?" he enquired and produced a box of worms, floats, sinkers etc and in no time I had four lovely trout and one whopper. When we rejoined the AOC he was amazed at my skill with the fly as the score was 5-0 to me and pointing to the whopper he asked what fly I had used. I told him the name of my unsuccessful fly and said that the whopper had just taken it hook, line and sinker. He looked at me with his quizzical smile and said, "Hook, line and sinker, Tony – I thought you were using a fly." 'I was, Sir, I just meant it metaphorically', but the SNCO gave the game away with his smirk and we ate the whopper for breakfast.

And then it happened. Out of the blue, the HQ was moving south to Leconfield near Beverley and Ouston was closing. I liked Ouston but Leconfield had two Hunter Squadrons, 19 and 92, and I felt that I was bound to get some Hunter flying and I did – lots. Leconfield was heaven for me except when I had nothing to do and the sky was blue and Hunters were breaking into the circuit all day; I felt like Casanova locked up in a cell overlooking the harem. So near yet so far and so many. Beverley was four miles away, a delightful small English market town and the locals asked me to shoot, to dinners and other parties; there were lots of daughters and very few eligible bachelors. At one party, at Watton Abbey, I met my future wife, Julia, courtesy of Christopher and Sally Firth who lived there. So, by an amazing twist of fate, because of John Volkers and I breaking all the low flying rules, I got my ADC's job and, after a 'whirlwind' romance lasting seven years, my wife. The RAF tried to switch ADCs and AOCs half way through each other's two years stint and it wasn't long before 'Mac' Maguire was posted away to higher ranks and a knighthood, which just goes to show how beneficial can be the effect of a good ADC on a senior officer's career. I was going to miss 'Mac' but his departure did not mean that I would take over his job - it meant another Air Marshal and he was going to have an uphill struggle to equal his predecessor in my affections.

Air Vice Marshal Gareth Clayton DFC was a very different personality. To his peer group he was universally known as Tubby, and he had a great sense of fun; a bomber pilot from the Second World War he had suffered numerous terrifying crashes. On one occasion he had been flying some friends down from Scotland to Wattisham in a Blenheim for a wedding and, when they arrived, there was thick fog and no means of communication available to them. Unable to find Wattisham, and with night approaching, he throttled back and landed straight ahead, blind, coming to a halt with hardly any damage in a field. On another occasion he took off in the back seat of a Meteor to do some instrument flying with a Wing Commander in the front cockpit; the Wing Commander said he would like to do a quick circuit as he was out of practice and, having taken control, rolled on some bank to turn downwind, stalled the aircraft and fell out of the sky from 600'. Gareth Clayton just had time to say "You stupid fool you have killed us both" before the wing slid into the ground, the aircraft broke up and 800 gallons of jet fuel exploded. Meanwhile in the cockpit, neither of them had a scratch on them and, when the fireball had subsided, they opened the hood and walked away unharmed. The biggest piece of wreckage was the cockpit.

In spite of these experiences and having used up eight of his nine lives, he was very keen on flying and, after a few days in his office, he came into mine and said "I'm bored Tony, let's go and fly the Meteor. You can sit in the back seat and make sure we are all right." It was against his rather inauspicious flying background that we went flying together for the first time. Leconfield had had its runway lengthened to 2500 yards a couple of years previously and the AOC 12 Group at the time had flown in a Meteor with his ADC, a navigator, in the back cockpit to celebrate the first landing on the new runway. He ran in for a break, deployed the airbrakes and, when the undercarriage was lowered, the aircraft pitched into the vertical leaving a large smoking hole and not much of the occupants. The AOC had rediscovered the Meteor's phantom dive. Airbrakes in wheels down, you lived; airbrakes out, wheels down, you didn't. We arrived at the HQ Flight where our Meteor awaited us. Gareth climbed in and flew quite a nice sortie until we turned downwind to land with the airbrakes out. Always keen to stay alive, I watched the airbrake lever while establishing a two handed lock on the undercarriage selector. Then, to my horror, the airbrake lever never moved but I felt huge pressure building up on my hands which I could hardly hold; the airbrakes were well out. A voice said "The undercarriage lever has jammed Tony," to which I replied "It hasn't Sir, I am locking it until the airbrakes are in." Oh Dear! The front cockpit erupted with uncomplimentary remarks about my duties, while the aircraft was turning and descending. We flew back diagonally over the airfield at 500' to the consternation of the staff in the control tower who said nothing about 'Hadrian's' unusual approach to flight in the circuit. After we had landed he never mentioned it again but we both knew I had saved our lives and that his invective had been a manifestation of shock. I thought it a good reason to have a pilot as an ADC and not, like the unfortunate AOC 12 Group, a navigator.

We started a round of visiting stations which I always quite enjoyed. These were informal visits to get to know the Station Commanders at each site together with the more important Wing Commanders and Squadron Leaders. It was always interesting to see the different approach adopted by the Group Captains to the man who could make or break their careers; these varied from the grovelling sycophant to the hale and hearty "We are all in this together." Some were professional and liked to keep the ADC very much onside in order to help themselves up the greasy pole. One of these was Group Captain X. Shortly before the annual AOC's inspection he rang me up for a chat. Most unusual. After some pleasantries, where he sympathised with my lack of flying, he asked if the new Air Marshal had any special things he liked to see. In fact, every time we had carried out an inspection, Gareth Clayton had asked for the bonnet to be raised on a specimen car in the MT section, which information I duly passed on. Come the great inspection we did the normal rounds after the morning parade and were running a little late for lunch when we arrived at the MT section; as we entered it the Group Captain introduced the AOC to the NCO in charge and then dropped back with me and gave a knowing look. The inspection went well and when he had finished he asked about the SNCO's family, but he never asked for a lift of the bonnet. The Group Captain glared at me and then, just as we were leaving, the AOC said "Just lift the bonnet on that Land Rover will you?" "Certainly, Sir," said the SNCO and the gleaming engine had to be seen to be believed. "Very good" said the AOC, "Just lift the next one will you?" Same result, but the icing on the cake came when he said "You might like to know, Group Captain, that this is the only unit that has cleaned both inside and out. Very good." I was so relieved; the Group Captain thanked me personally and was eventually promoted. It amazed me how such tiny things can give so much happiness but in my case it was just relief that my hot tip had come off. I heard from the Station Commander that the entire MT section had been cleaning engines all night. Later that day there was huge fun at the AOC's expense when a passing pigeon dropped a full war load right in the middle of his hat. Gareth Clayton thought it funnier than anyone and I was dispatched to have the hat cleaned to restore his dignity.

My flying now changed. Our ancient Anson was replaced with a de Havilland Devon, VP953, and as the AOC had spent all his formative years flying twin piston-engined aircraft he wanted to commute in it, not the Meteor. I did not mind too much as I was getting lots of Hunter flying from 19 and 92 Squadrons. The Devon was easy and viceless to fly but, like all aircraft, that did not prevent anyone, even an Air Marshal, getting into trouble. We had been to Aird Uig and took off from Stornoway, with 'the Captain' in the left seat, the faithful ADC in the right, and went straight into cloud; with all going well until the speed started falling off. By 8,000' we were still climbing, just, but with very high power settings. Ice was forming on the wings, flying off the propellers and cracking and banging into the fuselage. Then, at full power, we started descending. "Turn on the de-icing equipment, please, Tony." "We don't have any, Sir" I replied. We were heading metaphorically south into some nasty rocks; Stornoway had clamped and was unflyable but, to our relief, Tiree had an airfield and was still manageable; we turned back and made it, just. As the door opened, to our surprise a Flight Sergeant appeared. Our surprise was enhanced when the SNCO, replying to the AOC's question of which Command he was in, said "Fighter Command No.11 Group, Sir?" Gareth Clayton looked at me and said "It isn't ours is it Tony?" "No, Sir" I confirmed. But it was. There were six Air Force personnel to maintain a triangulation homer, and they were in 11 Group, but administered direct from Fighter Command HQ. We thought that we had discovered a lost tribe left over from WWII like some Japanese soldiers on a Pacific island. The weather stayed bad so we unloaded our fishing rods from the aircraft and spent two days fishing, staying in a little hotel as the only guests until, on Day 3, the weather cleared and we flew home. I actually managed never to mention that we could have been home in an hour on Day One in the trusty old Meteor. Occasionally the AOC and I would be asked to shoot on one or other of the large estates which abound in East Yorkshire. A day or two beforehand, as Gareth was on a no lunch diet, we would take our guns and a great many cartridges to a local clay pigeon set-up quite close to Leconfield. Gareth was adamant that we could not let the RAF down. No one is vulgar enough to count the birds he has shot at formal shoots but everyone knows which guns have missed most. The AOC felt that we should not disgrace ourselves or the RAF, especially as we came from the local fighter station which was home to all those legendary hot-shot pilots who were masters of deflection shooting - so we cheated and had a little practice.

Gareth Clayton did not really approve of my slipping off at lunchtime for a sortie with 19 or 92 Squadrons, it meant that I had an extended lunch break and no lunch. Then one day he decided that he was going to Fighter Command HQ and that I should stay behind, confined to the office, with no flying. All went well until 92 rang up to say that they were just going to launch a four-ship and would I like to be No. 4? The head of the harem had just rung up and asked Casanova if he could manage a quickie as the Sultan was out of town. I struggled into my flying kit while the briefing was going on and the four of us launched for the usual high level UK air defence sortie, 2 v 2 combat a tail chase and recovery. On returning to Leconfield the four-ship leader called us in to close for a formation practice over the airfield and then, to my horror, I heard "Hadrian 20 miles in bound" on the radio. My lead aircraft was flown by a very competent Pakistani, 'Raf' Rafiqi, and he wasn't put off by the AOC's return - but I certainly was. "Wing over port" "360 Starboard" went the lead. "Hadrian 10 miles" went Hadrian. I was in the box as No.4 and I had to stay there. The tower then told us to land as Hadrian was inbound so we broke off our four and landed; I taxied in, shut down, and sprinted over to 92. I tore off my flying kit, donned my uniform and drove the 300 yards to Group HQ at high speed, sprinted down the corridor and made it to my desk. At that moment I heard the boss coming down the passage and into his office. He pressed the buzzer and I entered. "Everything quiet while I have been away, Tony?" "Yes, Sir" He looked at me quizzically. "And how would you know? You have a great black mark on your face which more or less exactly follows the shape of a Hunter oxygen mask." I had been rumbled but he was very kind about this case of gross disobedience. On one other occasion I was in big trouble, very deep. It was the Group photograph at 2pm outside the Group HQ and 19 Squadron said I could fly a pairs sortie during lunch. I was No.2 to Bob Turbin and all went well until Patrington Radar called us to intercept a 'Zombie Raid' which was the usual Russian Bear reconnaissance. This seriously extended our sortie and, to cut a long story short, at 2pm the staff officers all took up their places for the photograph. Gareth noticed my absence. "Where's my ADC?" "I think he is flying," said a voice, and all Gareth said was "Is he indeed?" The Group photo appeared with me in a little box as 'absent' and this time I was grounded for a week.

It was in June 1962 that the AOC announced his summer holiday dates - a whole fortnight - and thus time for another check out on a new type. In the sixties RAF flying was easy going within Fighter Command but it was impossible to fly an aircraft belonging to Transport, Training or Bomber Commands if you were in Fighter. I had a longing to check out in a Canberra, one of the great classic twin-jet bombers. As luck would have it, however, the Central Fighter Establishment at West Raynham had three Canberras but they would never let me fly them either, unless I had completed the Canberra Ground School and passed a technical exam. The Canberra OCU was at Bassingbourn, near Royston, and they ran a weekly ground school but, being Bomber Command, would never let me near their aircraft. I wrote to the Wing Commander Flying at Bassingbourn (in Bomber Command) to say that I was due to fly a Canberra at the CFE and could I do the ground school with them. He said yes. Then I wrote to the Canberra Flight Commander at West Raynham, heading my letter 'From the ADC to the AOC 11 Group', to ask if I could fly a Canberra citing my twin time, my current instrument rating on the Meteor and saying that I could arrive for a week, having completed the Bassingbourn course. To my surprise and delight, he said yes. The time for the AOC's holiday came and to his enquiry whether I had anything special planned for my own break, I replied blandly "Nothing special, Sir", as I wasn't certain he would approve of my flying with 12 Group and I didn't dare risk mentioning it.

All went to plan. I passed the ground school and flew three duals and one solo; my logbook was stamped up as qualified on type, day only, and I was walking on air when I returned to Leconfield, especially when some of the other staff officers showed signs of jealousy. The Canberra had been a lovely, easy aircraft to fly in the low level general handling sorties that I flew, with the training emphasis on asymmetric flying and fuel management. August 1962 was the apex of my RAF flying career. After the Canberra conversion, and back at Leconfield, 92 Squadron lent me a Hunter and I flew to Middleton St George (Teeside) where I flew a dual in a Javelin T.3 and then another solo in the big Mk 9. I flew my usual Meteor sorties, flew some Cadets in a Chipmunk, some dual in the Anson and a few trips in the Devon with the AOC; a total of 21 hours on 6 types plus two variants in one month. If only the illegitimate Wing Commander could see my logbook.

The more you fly the more competent you become, but the dreadful numbers game starts to close in on you. Accidents. I had never had even an incident, had always within reason been as careful as I could be, and the RAF's cocooning system to protect very young and inexperienced pilots from themselves had kept me out of trouble. Until now. I was in the office and for once not flying when the phone rang - it was the boss. He was at the Fighter Command annual conference at the Central Fighter Establishment and needed some papers; I was to borrow a Hunter or Meteor and bring them down at once. 92 Squadron had a spare Hunter T.7, painted in the dark blue colour scheme of the Blue Diamonds aerobatic team, and in a very short time I tucked up the gear and set heading for West Raynham. I arrived very quickly and was much too heavy to land so I burnt off some fuel and then decided to do a practice Ground Controlled radar approach (GCA). All went well until I was about two miles out when the tower told me to land off this approach as they did not wish the noise of the go-around to disturb the conference. The wind was very strong right across the runway and I was very heavy, but only two hundred pounds over the limit and anyway I was solo in a two-seater. On 2000 yards the Hunter needs careful brake use to stop in good conditions but with a cross-wind of twenty knots I could effectively use only one brake so I put it down right at the end of the runway and applied maximum brake. The runway at West Raynham undulated and the end was not visible during the landing roll but, just as I was congratulating myself (as usual) on a skilful bit of flying, I topped the rise and saw the crash barrier three hundred yards in front of me and I still had 80 knots on. I went straight into the net and came to a rapid smooth halt. What a disaster. The whole flying demonstration for all the Air Officers in Fighter Command was cancelled because the blue Hunter that had been flown by the AOC 11 Group's ADC was snagged in the net. Sqn Ldr Mercer, who was boss of the Blue Diamonds was very displeased and I was humiliated, probably not before time. The Hunter was undamaged but I was.

Back in the office I occasionally had an insight into RAF discipline in action, or overheard interesting phone calls. We had a new Station Commander at Chivenor, a legendary Battle of Britain pilot with lots of kills, but after he had been at Chivenor for a week an agitated Wing Commander Admin rang up to talk to the Boss. Naturally someone like myself would never listen in on a conversation between two senior officers but sometimes one could not quite avoid it. The Wing Commander told the AOC that the new Group Captain, after a lunch time session in the bar, was lying on the floor of the Officers Mess with his dog licking his face. The AOC paused then said "Get him packed up, I am sending my Devon down for him. He is to be removed from Chivenor and taken to Fighter Command HQ." The man became a civilian that month. On another occasion an even more legendary Battle of Britain pilot, Denis Crowley Milling, rang up to say that he had been flying the Lightning at the CFE at West Raynham and, having forgotten to cancel the auto throttles, had gone into the barrier – he had my sympathy. He also said that, if it was not too late, that the RAF should only order two-seat Lightnings as the work-load in the single-seater was too high during intercepts. It was too late but many pilots who could fly the aircraft, which was easy enough, could not manage a weapons intercept as well and, when the Phantom arrived in service, they were then usually transferred to this aircraft which had a weapons man in the rear cockpit.

Sometimes I really enjoyed my duties as an ADC. The boss had completed a Hunter conversion at Chivenor before coming to his new post, but he had not flown one for several months and he announced his intention to refamiliarise himself - with me as safety pilot. Meteor memories came flooding back. He actually flew the aircraft quite well, once he had got it going but it took him thirty minutes from entering the cockpit to getting it started by using the published check-list and confirming every circuit breaker. Any normal Hunter pilot could have the aircraft running in 30 seconds. After a few trips the boss announced that we were going to Leuchars for a big lunch on Saturday. I was to fly as his No.2 in another Hunter so that, if his aircraft went unserviceable, he would take mine home. Once we had arrived I was told to accompany Dolores Hart, at the time a well-known film star, and what we would now call a 'celeb'. She was very pretty, our cold lobster lunch was wonderful (I managed a double portion) and by the end of the day, she knew just how brave fighter pilots were. Gareth Clayton's aircraft started; so did mine, and we left Leuchars for Leconfield as a very happy pair.

In spite of my rehabilitation, sort of, it was at Leconfield one evening that I got talking to an old fighter pilot and considered my future career. He had completed tours in Germany, in Iraq and at the CFE; in short he had been one of the top men in his profession. Then, with a shock that I can still remember, I realised that his life was over. He was in air traffic control and never flew; the scales fell from my eyes, and I saw the likely out-turn to my life if I stayed in the RAF. At that moment, I decided to leave. I think of it as my Damascene moment, but meanwhile there was flying to be done!

My relationship with the AOC was more like father and wayward teenager and on occasions we made each other very cross. One day I had extended my lunch hour a little too long and he had seen me coming back into the office. Usually I could get away with ten or fifteen minutes either side of my allotted hour but this time a little paternal chat was called for. "You must learn to get your priorities right, Tony. If you don't you will end up as a passed-over Squadron Leader. By the way we are going to Chivenor tomorrow so you had better get your hair cut – no, on second thoughts, don't, as it wouldn't suit you." I said nothing but what I was longing to say was that it was precisely because I was so heavily focussed on flying that we clashed; that flying was my priority - the sole raison d'être for everything I did and, after my report from Aden, as I was never going anywhere in the RAF I would in fact be leaving in eighteen months time! A week later I was having a chat with Marion, the AOC's wife, and I managed to say how much I loved the RAF and how sad I was to be leaving it. The message got home; the next day as GC came pounding down the corridor I was summoned at once. "What is all this about you leaving the RAF, Tony? You could have a great future if you stayed in." I thought he had it right the first time when he had said 'Passed-over Squadron Leader' and that presumed that I could pass my promotion exams otherwise it would be Passed-over Flight Lieutenant. I explained that I was a short service officer, as the contract was known, on an eight year engagement.

And then it was time for me to change jobs. The Claytons gave a dinner party to which I could ask seven guests; my future wife Julia, plus six.

When the dinner was over GC gave me a lovely pair of gold cufflinks and a choice of posting, within reason, for my last ten months in the RAF. I asked to go to the Hunter OCU at Chivenor and there I went, officially posted to the Meteor flight, but I could get more or less any flying that I wanted, and I did. My successor in this key military appointment as ADC was Dave Edmonston who had been a contemporary on 8 Squadron and then flown trials on the Harrier's forerunner, the Kestrel, at CFE. When Gareth Clayton had heard that his father, old Colonel Edmonston, owned a large part of Unst, the Island where Saxa Vord was situated, he had little hope of escape and was duly appointed, principally I thought so as to give the AOC privileged and legal access to the snipe shooting which was excellent on Unst, and to which sport he was particularly addicted.

A postscript

I started this chapter by saying that the relationship between a Senior Officer and his ADC is atypical of anything else in the service world that I encountered. To illustrate this I can only say that I have very few friends or contacts from my air force days, but, when they retired, I became close friends with both 'Mac' Maguire and Gareth Clayton. They both chose to retire within twenty miles of my home, as did the AOC's driver, Corporal Churchyard, until he emigrated to Australia. He is now Malcolm Churchyard, millionaire manufacturer of steel buildings in Queensland, Australia. Maguire set up an intelligence unit for Commercial Union and became a director, meanwhile Clayton ran the RAF Benevolent Fund, became a silversmith, with his own hallmark, and, most improbably, bought a trawler in partnership with a retired General. They took it in turns to be Captain or deckhand and eventually became principal contractors for harbour services to the Harwich Harbour Authority. When Clayton died his funeral was on a foggy day but, as the coffin was lowered into the grave, a lone Phantom appeared low over the scene and then, engaging its afterburners, disappeared vertically into the low cloud and mist. Wonderful symbolism and hardly a dry eye to be seen - certainly not mine.

Chapter 17

THE LAST TEN MONTHS ON HER MAJESTY'S SERVICE

After forty years I cannot reasonably expect Her Majesty to remember the excitement she must have felt as my time in her employment drew to a close. My non-flying ground appointment had allowed me an average of 20 hours a month and given me both a Javelin and Canberra conversion. The AOC said that he would try to post me to Chivenor, which he did. The RAF rules, however, had to be obeyed and, after a non-flying appointment, all pilots returning to flying duties had to undertake a thirty hour flying refresher course, at RAF Manby in Lincolnshire, on the piston-engined Provost. Never mind that I was posted to fly Meteors and Hunters, and my last three days as an ADC had given me six Hunter trips, the rules said that I needed basic flying training in the Piston Provost. More good news – I had never flown a Provost, so it was a new type and when, two years later, Adrian Swire offered me a trip in his Spitfire Mk IX he was more than happy that my Provost time was all that was needed to fly his aircraft safely. The refresher flying at Manby was meant to last four weeks but for the first fortnight the bitter winter of 1963 stopped all flying; in the second I flew 30 hours on the Provost, a handling pilot's dream with the most perfectly harmonised controls. It was and still is the best pure flying machine that I have flown but not the most exciting; looked at on the ground from head on it could easily be mistaken for a Föcke Wulf Fw190, a mistake I seemed to make every time I flew one. I completed my thirty hours and then packed my worldly goods, including my black Labrador, Jane, into my Ford Consul, and headed south for Royal Air Force Chivenor where, for the next nine months, I was either airborne or asleep. I had at last found a job in which I could spend all and every day flying so that even I had had enough and was bored only by the weekends.

The Meteor flight at Chivenor was established to tow banners for Hunter students to shoot at; each three month course included around ten days of air-to-air gunnery which meant that with three courses going through I was without a job for two months out of three. This presented no problems as the Meteor flight operated four single seat F.8s and one two seat T.7 with only four pilots on strength. In addition we were all Meteor self-authorising and could help out most days with Hunter sorties, leading students on their various exercises. In the eight months that I was at Chivenor I averaged just under 40 hours a month. Not all my flying was essential for the defence of the realm. An old school friend, Nick Rayner, was in the Army, serving in Northern Ireland and at two o'clock one Friday afternoon he rang me to ask if I could fly to Aldergrove, pick him up, fly him to Chivenor and drive him to his parents' home for a dance that evening; if I could, he added, I could go to the ball. I was airborne fifteen minutes later and landed at Aldergrove just over an hour after his telephone call; I unpacked his giant suitcase (Army officers have quaint ideas about the amount of room there is in a military jet) stowing his dinner jacket, pyjamas etc round the cockpit. The aircraft was refuelled very quickly and we landed back at Chivenor at 4.30 after a short aerobatic session, partly to show Nick the effects of 'G' but mainly because it seemed a pity to waste all that fuel. His family owned a big house in South Devon; we arrived in plenty of time and I drove a new girl-friend home in early daylight the next morning. Nick Rayner left the Army and joined Sothebys and eventually became their representative in Geneva. Handling the sale of the Duchess of Windsor's jewellery was one of the high points in his life, in fact probably second only to his flight in the Meteor.

On another occasion I impressed the 'Brown Jobs' in quite a different manner. I had been asked to shoot by an uncle in Suffolk and it seemed a pity to drive there when I could fly, so I packed my 12 bore, cartridges and weekend clothes into the ammunition bay of a single seat F.8 and forty minutes later landed at RAF Wattisham in Suffolk. A Land Rover had been sent to pick me up; I had a great weekend, missed even more birds than usual but, unfortunately, took more time to leave on Monday morning than I should have done, arriving at Chivenor at half-past ten instead of nine o'clock as planned. I needed to be back early as I had been tasked to escort a group of six Pongoes (Army) around Chivenor. They were quite impressed with life in the RAF when I climbed out of the Meteor in my country attire with my gun, cartridge bag, and a brace of pheasants to start my working week at ten thirty.

I decided to leave the RAF at my eight year point, on the grounds that

I had searched my kitbag for the mythical Field Marshal's baton that lies in every man's kit when he takes the Queens shilling; only mine seemed to be missing. I could have stayed for four more years but if I was going to leave I had to get on with it in order not to miss out on an alternative career - one that could not be ruined by one Senior Officer's annual report. I had had an amazing run of luck on the stock exchange and was paid a gratuity of £1500 to add to the £8000 that I had saved and multiplied; I also had a very wise and straight-talking uncle in Berkshire who seemed to have everything I aspired to. At this point I had thought of a career as a 'gentleman farmer', not too much work, plenty of shooting and no chance of getting my hands dirty. A rude awakening lay ahead.

Douglas Clavering was an agreeable personality and an RAF student on a long course; he had a brother in the Scots Guards and his parents owned the Sutherland Arms Hotel with plenty of country pursuits attached. He was clearly someone who could repay family hospitality so I arranged to spend a weekend with my Wellesley relations and, as Douglas was doing nothing, he came along too. Finding a quiet moment, I asked my uncle Dick Wellesley if he could give me some career advice as I was thinking of farming and he said that we would discuss it at the estate office the next morning at nine o'clock. We did and it was a pivotal moment in my life. He started by asking how much money I had. I included my gratuity and rounded my worldly wealth up to the magic figure of £10,000 of which I was inordinately proud as a twenty-five year old; a comfortable village house could be bought for £4,000 in those days so I felt rich. Uncle's face fell when he heard of my £10,000 and he asked me to describe my expectations and lifestyle when I was forty. After I had finished he said, "You poor boy, you cannot even think of farming you must go into the City and make some money – proper money. The wealth of the nation flows through every day and if none of it sticks to your palms then you do not deserve to have any." That was it, my careers officer had spoken and my future life pattern was set. There was a sad ending to the story. Douglas Clavering was posted to the Far East to fly Hunters in Singapore and disappeared while flying No.4 on a low-level battle sortie. No one saw him go, the flight was over the sea and suddenly there were three aircraft and not four. Meanwhile back at Chivenor I had a series of potentially life-threatening experiences.

One Friday after lunch a phone call from an engineering officer came through requesting that I pick up an airman from the CFE at West Raynham that afternoon. In no time at all the trusty two-seater Meteor T.7 was airborne. I climbed steeply to fly over the Green One airway that lay to the North of Devon the top of which was, in those days, 26,000'; the bottom was at 2,500' but the RAF did not acknowledge that and used 5,000'. It was a lovely day and I soon landed at West Raynham and found my man; he seemed a little nervous at the prospect of our flight together and in particular he wished to avoid any aerobatic manoeuvre. It transpired that he had only flown once before and that was in a two seat Hunter when, while flying a simulated 1-v-1 combat, his pilot had lost control, entered a spin, failed to recover and then ordered him to eject. I told him that there was no danger of ejecting from the Meteor T.7, as it was not fitted with ejection seats. Our flight home went well and as the weather was good I descended, flew down the North Devon coast at 1,000' and a mile off shore to avoid seagulls. The IAS read 360 knots when I saw a large black-backed gull about one second before there was a dull thud as if it hit the aircraft somewhere. I could see no damage but I had lost my airspeed indicator and had severe trouble moving the ailerons. Problems seldom happen singly and this one was compounded by my fuel state which was 40/40, or forty gallons a side, our normal minimum landing fuel. I pulled up and called for a priority straight-in approach with restricted controls and no air speed indication; I forgot to mention chronic fuel shortage. After landing I found a hole in the wing about 12 inches across and six inches deep, just invisible to me, outside the port engine nacelle, but, amazingly, there were feathers coming out of the wing through the rivet heads about four feet from the impact. The bird had gone through the leading edge and hit the main spar severing the ASI connection and bending the aileron rods; its remains had exploded horizontally along the main spar causing the whole structure to heave and thus allowing feathers to come out through the rivet heads. I have a photograph to prove it. A week later I flew the air test on the replacement wing now fitted to the T.7; as I reached unstick speed, but past the point at which I could stop, I found the left wing going down which I held, initially quite easily, but then as the speed increased so did the rolling moment. I reduced power and at 160 knots I could only hold the wing up by jamming my left elbow against the cockpit wall to stop the aircraft rolling inverted. I flew down-wind and landed well over the maximum landing weight but stopped before I went off the end of the runway. Apparently one aileron had been fitted upside down.

Having by now decided on a City career I had to find somewhere to work where I could make the million I needed to acquire a big house with a deer park and a few thousand acres. Eventually I obtained an interview with the merchant bank, Phillip Hill Higginson and Erlangers and, on the great day, I climbed into an F.8 and flew myself to Bovingdon in North London. There I recovered my smartest suit, whitest shirt and stiffest collar from the ammo tanks and caught the tube into London; I got off at the Barbican and walked down London Wall to the Moorgate intersection and soon found No. 34 Moorgate. I was to be interviewed first by the chairman, Sir Kenneth Keith and then by Derek Palmar (later Sir, and chairman of almost everything). Lord Keith later became chairman of Rolls-Royce. The bank was small but it took on one trainee a year; they did not mind what the trainee had done as long as it was something positive. Luckily 'fighter pilot' fell into this category. I told Palmar that I was free on the 1st April, this being September, and he told me he would get in touch. I took the train to Bovingdon, wound up my Meteor and flew home to Chivenor.

I am a very impatient person and every day I expected a letter, but nothing came so, after a fortnight, I decided to write and tell Mr Palmar that I could now start work on January 1st and that I looked forward to doing so. I received a letter by return of post saying that I could start on January 1st at £750 per annum which was exactly half my RAF pay but, whereas my board and lodging were free in the Air Force, I was now going to have to cover these myself while living in London. It was 'welcome to the real world' and it was also welcome to a small problem - the RAF had no idea that I was leaving on December 31st, 1963 and I could hardly just go AWOL. I asked for an interview with the Group Captain Station Commander and told him that I had been offered a fantastic job in the City provided, and only provided, that I could start work on January 1st. It was a bit like organising my Canberra and Javelin checkouts and it worked – I received a letter saying that I would be released on the date I wanted. I heard later that Derek Palmar interviewed seven people all told and then waited to see who pushed and who didn't. Luckily my impatience made me push and the bank wanted 'pushies'.

Meanwhile back at Chivenor I had more flying to do and another near miss which was entirely my fault. It had been decided to train army officers in the art of Forward Air Controlling, the role that had sent 8 Squadron pilots up-country with the army, and this task was given to the Meteor Flight. It required lots of low level high-speed flying and some accurate navigation with a map. I had flown several of these sorties and then, on one of them, the army radio failed so the exercise was cancelled. Flying aerobatics in the F.8 with fuel in the ventral tank was not permitted, so I pulled out the airbrakes and went to a high power setting to burn off the ventral fuel. After a few minutes I glanced down at the fuel gauges to see the dreaded 40/40 minimum landing state and I was a good thirty plus miles from home. I shut the airbrakes converted my speed to height and shut down one engine; I made it but to this day I can remember praying that I did not flame out while taxiing in - I didn't but there was no fuel left. The last thing I needed was an ejection two months before my departure from HM's employ. What had made me look down at that precise moment I will never know, but I was very relieved as a minute later would have been too late. For some unknown reason the ground crew had decided not to fill the ventral tank for that sortie and I had not checked the paperwork before take off. It had been my fourth sortie of the day and I was flying and operating in an automatic mode and suffering from both over-familiarity and confidence.

And then it was over. My boss was Squadron Leader 'Buck' Ryan who had been at 11 Group HQ with me and, in the middle of November, he called me in and grounded me forthwith. I was given some very boring jobs to do one of which was a pay parade. I took my Labrador with me and walked up to Station HQ to collect the money which was in a canvas bag; the old dog asked to carry it and she trotted along beside me with the bag in her mouth until we arrived at the hangar where the airmen and NCOs were standing in ranks waiting for their money. I turned to the dog who gazed at me adoringly and wagged her tail but the money-bag had gone. In a panic I had the parade dismissed with instructions to reform an hour later; lied to the NCOs, saying that I thought they had the money and, in a real state, retraced my footsteps making the usual encouraging noises to persuade the dog to find the cash. She did, under a bush where she had put it. I had started my career by losing my rifle – it was pleasingly symmetrical to lose the airmen's wages at the end of it. Both offences could or would have resulted in a mandatory Court Martial and my city career would have been finished before it had begun.

I started packing up and going through the 'clearing procedure' demanded when leaving any station; this still entailed walking round every section to ensure that the leaver is not retaining any Air Force property and it takes, or took, all day. I hated it but the dog loved it. Everything was fine except for a set of Chipmunk Pilot Notes which I had lost and for which I had to pay half-a-crown which would now be an inflation adjusted £2; it took me an extra hour to pay the money and finish with the Royal Air Force. As I drove away from Chivenor a pair of Hunters on a low level sortie came unseen from behind and disappeared into the distance a second later. It was a symbolic farewell and I had a lump in my throat.

Chapter 18

THE TIGER CLUB

When I was eighteen, and before I joined the RAF, I had become a member of the Royal Aero Club at 119 Piccadilly. I had seldom used it, other than for lunch and the occasional night stop, but where else could an air-mad teenager lunch with Sir Geoffrey de Havilland and Sir Frederic Handley-Page at the adjoining table, as I did one day. By January 1964 my glittering Air Force career was over the RAeC had lost its premises at 119 Piccadilly and merged with the Lansdowne Club in Berkeley Square: this had little to recommend it, other than its squash courts, and there one day I played, and lost, to Martin Barraclough. As I settled into life in the City I had decided never to fly again but Martin, who also worked in the City, and was in Shipping, thought that I would enjoy the Tiger Club at Redhill in Surrey, and so that Sunday I drove my little red Mini to Redhill to see what it was all about. As I got out of my car I saw an aircraft take off to the North while, across the top of the airfield, inverted at around 300', flew a biplane which then performed a flick roll from the inverted to the inverted. I was amazed.

The Tiger Club had been formed and financed by Norman Jones to encourage sporting aviation, mainly aerobatics and racing; it was run by his son Michael, who, I felt, was never making quite the best use of his degree from Oxford. Michael gave me some forms to fill in and told me that I would have to have an acceptance check-ride in a Tiger Moth with the Chief Pilot, Neil Williams, he who I had just seen flying totally irresponsibly over the airfield, even though I must admit I had been quite impressed. Neil, incidentally, crashed at the Biggin Hill air show flying the same inverted flick manoeuvre a year later, and, miraculously, was only bruised even though he and his seat were the largest objects in the wreckage. The accident was recorded by the commentator John Blake in his inimitable style, "and Neil has taken it down behind the hangars." Thump, cloud of dust. "...and he has left it behind the hangars." I left for London and as I had never flown a Tiger Moth decided that I had better cheat a little before my test flight and spend some money on a little instruction in the Tiger Moth at Fairoaks in Surrey. This I did and then presented myself at Redhill for my check ride with Williams. He gave me a hard time and, finally, when we landed said, somewhat brutally, that for someone who had never flown a Tiger before it wasn't too bad.

A few days later the post arrived at 9 Cheyne Place. There was a letter from the Tiger Club. I was 'in' and that Saturday drove down to Redhill and was immediately pounced on by James Baring who had been in the RAF section of the School Corps with me. James thought I should fly as boxman in the team of four Turbulents that he led; 'the Turb' was powered by a Volkswagen engine but alas I was much heavier than the other three pilots. My trial for the team was a disaster as a little vic of three aircraft climbed away leaving me two or three hundred feet low on them - not quite Red Arrows stuff so I was fired. It was springtime and the Tiger Club was gearing up for its summer displays. Neil Williams needed a No.3 man for his tied together act which he led with Martin Barraclough as his No.2. This was extremely demanding flying and, as we got better and better, Williams flew it tighter and tighter until I can honestly say that it was the most knuckle clenching, demanding flying that I have ever done but huge fun and enormously satisfying. In the hangar at Redhill was one of the prettiest shapes, the Cosmic Wind 'Ballerina'; one of three built in America to the design of Tony le Vier, Lockheed's then Chief Test Pilot. The Cosmic, as it was known, was only flown by Peter Phillips and Neil Williams. Peter, a Hunter man, I had met in the RAF briefly in 1958, and Neil I had met and talked the night away in Aden. However, this common factor in our backgrounds counted for nothing. Norman had asked them to fly it and they were determined to keep it to themselves. About a year later a miracle happened – Norman asked me if I would like to fly the Cosmic Wind.

The aircraft was a sheer delight with very light controls and a fantastic rate of roll. On an inverted flick roll the rate of roll had been recorded at 400° per second using the frame counting technique with a slow motion camera. Its handling was not unlike a Hunter but without the power and inertia. After I had had my fill I taxied in to see the gaunt figure of Peter Phillips glaring at me and not looking very happy at all: it transpired that he and Neil had refused to fly the Cosmic until Norman replaced the safety harness and, as there was no-one else allowed to fly it, the aircraft was grounded. Norman craftily failed to mention this so I flew it with a clear conscience and, after a couple more trips, took it to Shoreham for a display. It was an amazing design, beautiful to look at with an amazing performance. At one air show I started my act with 360 mph indicated and all on the same engine as in my little Piper Cub, a 100hp 'Continental'.

The Tiger Club filled my life at weekends; during the week at the bank I actually enjoyed learning about money, if not the job itself, and in the evenings I laboured over my Institute of Bankers examinations. At Redhill there were lots of aeroplanes to fly and very congenial company from which I made lifelong friends. Tom Storey was one of these. He had just qualified as a chartered accountant and then taken a year off to design, build and fly his own aircraft. It had Union jack wings and tail and a little note on the back saying 'made in Japan' as in those days everything was, much as it is in China today. Tom flew it a few times and then asked if I would like to fly it. 'Just take it up, stall it, and see what you think.' I did as I was told and on landing was greeted with 'What is the stall like?' I had become a test pilot! At that time the Labour government had just cancelled the TSR.2 so Tom called it the TSR.3 – Tom Storey Racer 3, or, as it was known colloquially, the Wonderplane.

The little Volkswagen-powered Turbulent was a delight to fly and very cheap to operate so on some weekends, when flying was over, I took one home to Horsey Island, usually routing via Rochester and then, at very low level, through the Southend Danger Zone which I knew was never active at weekends. One day I was flying home up the coast when an enormous column of water erupted to two or three hundred feet off my right wing tip. I had forgotten that I was going home on a Monday when the Zone was active. On another occasion Norman Jones asked me to fly a Turbulent on floats which John Urmston had made for him. We flew it up to Horsey Island, I became a float plane pilot, and wrote an account of this for Vintage Aircraft Magazine and, as I was not paid, and the magazine has been defunct for many decades, I have included it at Appendix III as it captures the enthusiasm and atmosphere of Redhill in those days.

After a year Neil Williams persuaded me to join him in the competitive aerobatic world and introduced me to an RAF Squadron Leader 'Taff' Taylor. Taff had spent several years at the Central Fighter Establishment and the three of us started intensive flying on the Stampe, a lovely Belgiandesigned biplane with all the bad points of the Tiger Moth eliminated, despite its superficial similarity to Sir Geoffrey's legendary creation. One day I suggested that we bought a Jungmeister which would be much more manoeuvrable and had greater power. As soon as I mentioned this, Neil said "No, we must buy a Zlin 226." This was the latest East European aerobatic aircraft and one that could be flown by an aspiring world champion, he said. Neil was short of money because he had a wife and family to look after so Taff and I said we would buy it and in no time at all Neil was off to Belgium to collect it. There was heavy snow in January 1965 and there was only one movement at Gatwick, our Zlin, inbound for Customs clearance; five miles to the North a group of Tiger Club pilots awaited Neil's arrival. Darkness fell so we put out eight little gooseneck flares and then, magical moment, out of the night came Neil and Zlin landing on the snow, where we had compacted it, by the light of our eight little goosenecks. God knows how he even found the aerodrome.

That started my aerobatic flying. Neil was then a test pilot at Farnborough and the aircraft went there to be stripped of anything and everything that was not essential; so out came batteries, starter, generator etc. Also, off the inboard leading edge of the wing came small triangular bits of metal fitted to make the stall/flick combination gentler; a gentle stall was the last thing we needed. Finally the Zlin went into the paint shop to emerge in a striking colour scheme designed by Neil's artistic brother Lynn. With the paperwork straight the CAA man was invited to inspect it and, according to Neil, it was important that he be allowed to find something wrong. When the surveyor had finished he stood back and announced that it was a fine aircraft in fine condition with fine paperwork – however there was no placard fitted in the cockpit prohibiting smoking. Neil put his hand in his pocket, produced a small 'No smoking' sticker, and stuck it on the instrument panel. The aircraft was thus cleared for test and Neil persuaded the CAA to let him fly the test rather than one of their own pilots. The reason for this was simple – with those little triangular stall breakers removed the aircraft would fail any official test flight and with them refitted we couldn't compete. As the surveyor had not noticed their absence we competed! The next world championships were in Moscow and scheduled for August 1966 so we had fifteen months to prepare and for fifteen months Taff Taylor and I drove to Farnborough, every weekend, stayed with Neil and Jean, and flew and flew and flew. During the summer one of us would sometimes take a day off and use a Tiger Club Stampe to raise money from air shows; I organised these and kept the accounts. At the end of our Moscow trip we had paid for all our training and we each had a cheque for £225 equivalent to around £3,500 today.

I didn't like competition aerobatics. They gave me dreadful headaches on Monday and Tuesday which gradually faded away until, by Friday, they had gone; but then it was Saturday again. The worthy citizens of Farnborough put up with our endless droning, saving only one retired senior officer who complained direct to the Group Captain every weekend. One Sunday the Group Captain asked us not to fly until he said so. Around eleven o'clock he rang to say we could go; he had waited until the phone rang with the noise complaint and from then on he could ignore the complainant, as he knew we had been on the ground.

For fifteen months training at Farnborough was my total preoccupation. I had been dumped by my girlfriend (I eventually married her) but there was still time for 'romance' in the London of the swinging sixties and if a 27 year-old bachelor had any lack of 'love' problems at that time then he certainly had problems; London in those days was a target rich environment for any bachelor! Charles Boddington and Barry Tempest were two pilots who had flown in the British team in years past and presumed they would do so again in 1966. So the Royal Aero Club insisted that a selection contest be flown as a consequence of which Charles and Barry were dropped. The team that resulted consisted of Neil, Taff Taylor and me flying the Zlin, with Robin d'Erlanger and James Black flying the Stampe. Everyone was worried that Neil would not be allowed to go to Moscow as he had been doing some development flying of the TSR.2's radar. In the event, to our amazement, the Air Ministry cleared Neil and myself but blocked Taff Taylor without a second's pause; over dinner I found out why. Taff and I were discussing amazing things that we had seen and his contribution was the description of an H-Bomb detonation which he photographed from a U2 spyplane he was flying. This was the first time he had ever mentioned his secret attachment to the CIA under cover of an exchange tour with the USAF. He left me longing for more but said only that on one of his last flights from Beale AFB in California he had spotted the most amazing aircraft that anyone could imagine. He would say no more but seven or eight years later the SR-71 Blackbird was unveiled. When I saw my first SR-71 picture I knew what he had been talking about.

We had very few excitements during our training but there were one or two. One day at full power I found myself in a flat inverted spin right over the middle of Farnborough at around 11-1200'; the rate of rotation was unbelievable but, reducing power dropped the nose, and opposite rudder and stick back killed the spin with 3 or 400' to spare. Neil was worried that I was going to break the aeroplane and spoil his chances of being world champion; I was more worried about myself. Two days before our departure for the Kremlin I was ferrying the aircraft to Redhill when a piston disintegrated. Luckily I could just glide to Redhill. Although this was my third engine failure I found - and still do - an engine failure to be an attention-grabbing moment. "Williams Works Wonders" was the quote of the day when a team from Farnborough worked through the night to produce us a fully functioning aircraft by the next morning.

I thoroughly enjoyed the flight up to the Baltic and then, via Poland, to the USSR. Poland looked as if it was trapped in a nineteenth century time warp. We saw no cars, no power cables, or any of the things that the 20th century had done in the west to ruin its landscape; the countryside drifted past with trees and lakes and stately homes. Eventually I saw a great weal in front of us right where the border between Poland and Russia was marked on the map, and corresponding exactly to it. It must have been 100 metres wide and was devoid of any vegetation; quite clearly fraternal intercourse between Russians and Poles was discouraged. Then we flew a low slow journey to Moscow, escorted by a huge Russian AN-2 biplane, along a route redolent with the history of the Second World War. Vitebsk, Minsk and Smolensk had previously been just names in history books to me. We night stopped at Minsk at a hotel that made a Travelodge motel look five star; I took a bath during which the door opened – there was no lock - and a very old grizzled woman entered with a towel and made little attempt to avert her gaze from my manhood. Everyone in Minsk spoke pidgin German, presumably picked up during the war, and I dare say my elderly crone had seen a German or two; I only hoped I measured up to her expectations. While we were en route England won the World Cup at football of course; I am ashamed to say that I had no idea it was even on or that it was of any significance. The Soviets looked after us very well: there were parties with astronauts, a comfortable room at the Junost hotel and, if it hadn't been so hot, it would have been a very enjoyable holiday.

Down at the airfield everything was very efficient. Each nation had a tent drawn up in a huge open-sided square. At the centre of the square, side by side, were the tents for the East and West Germans. The only fault in the otherwise perfect organisation was an absence of loos so it was agreed that everyone would pee behind the German tents. Robin D'Erlanger decided to impress the Russians with the superiority of Western technology; he had the latest Western wonder, a mobile shaver with a battery/plug-in option. He spent some time searching the ground outside the Russian tent until he had a curious audience at which point he plugged his razor into the earth and (on battery power of course) started shaving. And then it was all over; the Russians won. I would like to say 'Surprise, surprise' but they were much the best. Neil came 14th, and I was 31st out of 64, and we all flew home.

After Moscow everything was rather anticlimactic and I needed a holiday. One of the other three executive trainees at the bank was David Buik who, nowadays, can be heard reviewing the markets for the BBC at some incredibly early hour. He needed a holiday too so I hired a two-seat, side-by-side, Jodel Mascaret from the Tiger Club, and we set off to fly to Marrakesh, in Morocco. We flew to Gatwick to clear customs and then direct to Bordeaux for French 'Douane', followed by a short hop to Biarritz for a night stop. The next day I nearly killed us both through arrogant stupidity. There was a great belt of cloud across central Spain but Gibraltar was clear so I decided to climb to a safe height and route through the cloud direct to Gibraltar at 10,000'. I did not have an instrument rating or even a radio licence, having just failed the civil test. All went well for an hour or so until we started to ice up. I needed more and more power to maintain first speed and then height. To maintain our height I had to cancel the carburettor heat in the hope that carburettor icing would be less likely at a high power setting – something that I had heard. It may have been less likely but it still happened. The engine started coughing and spluttering and then we were heading earthwards, with high ground underneath us, whether we liked it or not. I just managed to keep the engine going as we descended and then, suddenly, we popped out of cloud in a valley with mist on the hills to left and right. My poor passenger, not realising how close to death we had been asked where we were. I explained that I had had a change of plan and that we were heading East to Valencia for lunch. The Valley ran eastwards and I was going towards better weather. When I hit the coast I would fly south until Valencia turned up; I did and it did. After lunch we took off and headed down the coast and round the corner to Gibraltar where I slept quite exceptionally well. A few years later Neil Williams died in a Heinkel III, together with three others, when he too made an error of judgment in Spain and flew into the head of a valley in similar weather. I was lucky – he wasn't.

We had decided to stay at the La Mamounia hotel, Marrakech's largest and smartest - and as patronised by Sir Winston Churchill himself. The targets were the bored daughters of rich men who needed a little holiday romance, and to hell with the expense. Arriving hot and sweaty at 3pm we were politely (sort of) shown the door, as we had not booked. Eventually we found an Arab 'doss house', the Hotel d'Alger, where rooms cost one shilling and sixpence a night but billionaires' daughters seemed to be conspicuous by their absence. The next day we hired two bikes for one shilling each and cycled round the old town and out to a few villages. We saw 633 Squadron in French which had done little to improve an already dreadful film; declined to buy a cheque for 100,000 Canadian dollars face value with 'annulé' written all over it, and continued to decline to buy it when the price was down to £10.We also passed up an invitation from two hideous backpacking, left-wing Australian Sheilas, whose fathers were definitely not billionaires, to join them. Marrakech was a wonderful place but after three days we flew to Casablanca where the French sub-culture was all-pervasive and we experienced our first earth tremor - terrifying. We then flew home via Tangier, Gibraltar, Cognac and Caen. We flew straight across the Channel and were routed to Gatwick via several beacons, which I had to find by map reading as we had no VOR equipment in the aircraft, and then finally to Redhill. As a postscript the Mascaret we flew was wrecked the next year on the Yorkshire moors when it crashed due to engine failure induced by carburettor icing.

Eventually one day when David Buik and I were manning the treasury desk at Hill Samuel the phone rang for me. It was a Wednesday morning early in 1967,and a voice asked me if I would be prepared to fly a Hunter again in Saudi Arabia. I explained that I was now a high-powered merchant banker (clerk in the treasury), but then the voice said what he was paying for a fourteen month contract, tax-free and all found - I told him to hang on. I popped next door and asked Dolf Mootham the banking director if I could leave at once and he said "Of course" - rather too quickly I thought - so back into my office I picked up the phone and said, "OK." I was told to report to Chivenor that night to fly the simulators on Thursday and then go to RNAS Yeovilton on Friday to fly two sorties in the Hunter T.7, (although it turned out to be the Navalised T.8) and then, on Saturday morning, I flew to Jeddah. On Sunday I arrived at Taif, a Royal Saudi Air Force base East of Mecca in the Hijaz Mountains and on Monday I flew a pairs sortie. One of the advantages of being single is the speed with which decisions can be made!

Chapter 19

MAGIC CARPET

Airwork Services and British Aerospace had signed a big defence contract with the Royal Saudi Air Force. This had been negotiated in great haste after the Egyptian Air Force had bombed a village on the southwestern corner of Saudi Arabia where it borders with Yemen. The contract's purpose was to provide six Hunters and six Lightnings, together with their supporting air and ground crews, for a two year period, at a new RSAF airbase that was being constructed at Khamis Mushayt, fifty miles north of the Yemen border. However as it was Airwork's policy not to employ mercenaries, and the RSAF would not enrol non-nationals, the twelve pilots were contracted to a Mr Geoffrey Edwards who had negotiated the so called 'Magic Carpet' contract: Edwards in his turn sub-contracted Airwork to pay and administer his pilots. A neat pragmatic resolution.

Dickie Elliman and I arrived on Sunday evening at Taif, via Jeddah, to make up the contracted number of six Hunter pilots. Airwork had been paid for six but so far only provided four; the RSAF were not pleased, hence the panic rush to get me re-familiarised and out to Arabia within four days. Dickie had been a Javelin pilot in Germany and had little Hunter time so, on the first Monday morning, the Hunter Flight Commander, Terry Oldham, took me as his No.2 in a pair of F.6s and we flew to Riyadh, the capital of Saudi Arabia; I forget why. There I met the Lightning pilots most of whom had no previous type experience and for whom Airwork had had to pay the RAF £80,000 each for their training, equivalent to £1m now. Terry and I spent the night in the Military Academy at Riyadh, an appalling concrete structure on the far side of the airfield. I loved both Taif and Khamis but mercifully only ever spent that one night in the Saudi capital; in the evening I walked out onto the airfield and sat down alone, on a stone, as the sun went down. There is often a stillness at sundown and, when there is, it is a magical moment; from far across the desert airstrip I could hear the muezzin call the faithful to prayer, a sound that brought memories of my time on 8 Squadron flooding back. As I returned to my quarters in the dusk I suddenly wondered at what I had done and where my future lay. At the age of 29, a year as a mercenary fighter pilot, currently unemployed, would not look very impressive on my curriculum vitae when I returned to the real world.

We flew back to Taif and still had plenty of fuel on arrival so, while Terry landed, I broke off and indulged myself in some jet aerobatics, so different from those I had flown in the Zlin. The 'bingo' lights soon illuminated showing that I was now down to 1300 lbs of fuel and ought to be landing so I turned for home and ran up the airfield at an exhibitionistic 500 feet and 500 knots. Rolling on the bank I pulled a healthy amount of G and then, without warning the Hunter 'pitched up', an uncontrolled and sudden increase in the turn rate due to the wing tips losing lift. This should not happen and, as I walked back from the aircraft, I wondered if I had been ham-fisted when initiating the break. A fortnight before I had arrived an RSAF pilot who had been flying one of the Hunters had pitched up on finals, stalled and been killed. The accident had been attributed to pilot error but now I wondered if the Centre of Gravity in my aircraft had been a little far aft. In the Hunter the CG moves aft with the expenditure of ammunition and, when the guns have fired out, the CG is on the aft limit. I then found that the Hunters in Taif had no radar ranging unit in the nose and, without any ammunition, or ballast in lieu, the aircraft was flying outside its design limitations. It was almost certainly this that had killed the Saudi pilot. I kept quiet not wishing to compromise the Airwork contract and ballast was fitted.

Two days later Mike Perkins and I left the very long Taif runway for some practice one-v-one air fighting. As I turned in on him he broke hard into me, climbing and turning to prevent my getting a sighting shot, when out of his aircraft came a great long white trail of smoke; smoke that I had last seen from Manx Kelly's Hunter when he was hit in the Upper Yaffa district of Aden. I could almost see the exclamation mark over Mike's cockpit, then a voice said "I've flamed out." I knew he had, the white smoke was unburnt vaporising jet fuel. The engine would not relight and Mike executed a perfect dead stick landing back at Taif with me on his wing. A week later the aircraft was ready for test and Mike and I haggled over who was to do it; my argument was that he had shown that he could handle a flame-out for real, and was in practice, so I flew the chase plane. Thank heavens. The T.7 flamed out again and Mike did another copybook landing, making two in a week. The trouble was the same that I had experienced as a trainee student at Chivenor, and to which the 100 series Avon was prone, namely a malfunction of the unit that reduces the amount of fuel supplied at altitude; technically the BPC unit.

Taif was a lovely airfield, high in the mountains, so it was cool and dry. Adjacent, and lending its name to the RSAF fighter station was the old mediaeval city of Taif, made largely of big buildings with thick walls to keep cool, or warm, depending on the season. The souk, or market, was busy and thriving, the Arabs delightful and friendly (as long as you were not Jewish), and had not then acquired their distressing interest in cutting the throats of infidels, preferably while being filmed. Flying provided all the excitement that I needed without having my throat cut while I was out shopping. The plan, however, was to move us down to the new air base at Khamis Mushayt, a little short of two hundred miles south of Taif. Around three weeks after I arrived, Col. Rais, RSAF, arrived to brief us and announce that Khamis, with the exception of the fire services, was ready to receive the Hunters. The fire services would not be ready, or available, for another month but we were to take four Hunters to Khamis the next morning.

Terry Oldham, the Flight Commander, called a meeting of the pilots and, he unilaterally declared, that we were unanimous in our decision not to fly without a fire crew. Terry went to see Col. Rais to give him the news, was fired, and told to be on the 2 o'clock Hercules flight to Jeddah. "Send in the next Flight Commander," said the Colonel. This was Dan Carter, a very old Airwork pilot. The same thing happened. "Now Mr Dan I want the Hunters to fly to Khamis tomorrow." Dan was a really nice man but not capable of individualistic thought. "You heard what the Flight Commander said, Sir. No fire trucks, no flying." "Right Mr Dan, send in the next Flight Commander. You are sacked and can join Mr Terry on the 2 o'clock Hercules." It was decided that I was the next Flight Commander, so in I went. "Right Mr Tony I want the Hunters at Khamis tomorrow." "Fine, Sir," I replied, "what time do you want us there?" "On the ground at 10 o'clock." "We'll be there, Sir" -and we were. I had only gone to Saudi Arabia to increase my meagre capital and I wasn't going to throw away such an opportunity just to show solidarity with my fellow workers. The other three agreed to stay with me and at half past nine the next day our four Hunters were airborne. We gave Taif a farewell fly-by and, with a touch of apprehension, I turned the four south and headed for our new base on the edge of Indian Territory. I say apprehension because I was not in practice at 420 knot low-level navigation, we had no aids of any sort at Khamis and flight over rock and sand is not easy until you are used to it. We were two minutes from a major international incident if I screwed up by violating Yemeni airspace. I didn't. We taxied in and shut down; Col. Rais met us and pronounced us operational as No.6 Squadron Royal Saudi Air Force and formally put me in charge of it. It wasn't a very big command but certainly more than I would have been given by the illegitimate RAF Wing Commander who I hoped was still back gently rotting at the Ministry of Defence.

The Base Commander at Khamis was Colonel Sammi Saud, a delightful avuncular figure, who, I was assured many times, had flown Vampires. At the end of every day, if we wished to fly on the 'morrow, I had to go to the Colonel's office and wait my turn for an audience. Anyone and everyone had a right to be heard and I used to take my turn behind angry neighbours, disillusioned goat herdsmen, compensation seekers and any one else who wished to see him. This right of access to the boss by anyone slows life down in the Middle East but seems to be a common custom throughout the Arab and Jewish worlds. Eventually it would be my turn. "I would like to fly two Hunters tomorrow Colonel." "Certainly, but I want a beat up," was the invariable reply. Having frequently been in trouble doing unauthorised fly-bys in the RAF I now found them a nuisance, and our training suffered. Luckily the Russian/Egyptian axis at Sanaa was bent on defeating the Royalists within the Yemen and this gave us six months to work up before they crossed the border into Saudi airspace. There were, nevertheless, a few incidents during this time. On one occasion the Egyptian Airforce bombed a Red Cross convoy with poison gas leaving only one survivor. This gentleman, very ill indeed, was strapped onto a stretcher in the back of a Douglas DC-3 'Dakota' to be flown to Jeddah and thence home; the DC-3 was then caught in a sandstorm and crashed. All aboard were killed except the guy in the back on the stretcher who was the only survivor- for the second time in three days. We flew several sorties looking for the wreckage but never found it and some Bedouin eventually carried the poor man to a Saudi army base where he survived and returned to civilisation.

I started playing bridge in the school holidays when I was eleven or twelve as there was no television at home in the late forties: at Khamis Mushayt when we were not flying or on standby, we played bridge. I kept a record of my winnings and in the eleven months I was there these totalled just over £1,200, or the equivalent of £15,000 today. While working in the city I had made virtually nothing off a huge turnover on the stock market. The government had made a pile from taxing my transactions, my broker also made a pile; the market maker - or jobber as they were known in those days - made another small fortune while I, the luckless punter, made very little indeed! Stupidly, shortly before leaving Hill Samuel, I fancied a rather dodgy insurance company and decided to back it. I sold every share I owned, realising just over £11,000; then I rang the Chairman, a Mr Hunt I seem to remember, and told him that I was buying 12000 of his shares at around 90p each (although in those days it was eighteen shillings and three pence) and asked him for his views on the prospects of his company. He told me that he had several million shares and if I wanted to get rich I should stick with him. I did, and I kept a graph on the wall of my room in Khamis with the daily valuations marked up from the rather late air mail editions of the Daily Telegraph. My saw-toothed graph climbed steadily which gave me huge pleasure in three ways; first, because I was making a pile, secondly because as long as I stayed abroad for a full tax year I would pay no capital gains tax, and thirdly because it pissed off one of the Lightning pilots, an ex naval officer, who I thoroughly disliked. When the shares reached £2 each I wrote a letter to my broker instructing him to sell but, by the time he received the letter and sold them, they stood at £2.20. The Vehicle and General Insurance Company went bust a year later; just before it did so the shares were over £4 each. I had been lucky to sell when I did. I had only gone to Saudi to enrich myself (relatively) but my bridge winnings, my pay and the stock market had added at today's values close to £300,000. My hobby was flying, and the Hunters came free, as did my board and lodging so, with the taxman avoided due to my non-resident tax status, my eleven months actually in Arabia really paid off.

Meanwhile back at base, as they say, Vaughan Radford had arrived from the RAF. He had been on 8 Squadron in Aden and longed for the mercenary life and its rewards, so he resigned his commission. As an ex-Cranwell graduate the RAF refused to release him. A month or so later however, the

Group Captain at Khormahsar in Aden posted a notice to say that anyone who paid their mess bill with a cheque that was dishonoured would be court martialled and dismissed the service. Vaughan told his bank to dishonour any cheque drawn on his account and waited. Summoned before his Station Commander he was told that he had fooled nobody by his actions but would be court martialled before he could leave the Service. Although he came to Saudi as the designated CO of the Lightning flight at Khamis he flew Hunters with us to start with as we were short of pilots. When our contract ended the RSAF retained Vaughan as their adviser on fighter operations and acquisitions and he eventually moved to Washington on the staff of the Saudi Arabian embassy.

We were now responsible for the air defence of South West Arabia by day: by night defence consisted of a Hawk Surface-to-Air Missile battery. The Saudi army looked after the Hawk system, supplied by the Americans, and it was their custom to sleep through the night until dawn. One night by the light of a full moon, they were rudely awakened by exploding bombs. The Egyptian Air Force had bombed the SAM site from 20,000' in full moonlight. Justice was swift. The unfortunate duty crew were collected by Hercules the next day, flown to Riyadh and shot - or so we were told by our Colonel. No multi-million pound enquiries with multiple appeals to enrich m'learned friends; just death. An excellent legal system. Thereafter our free and easy life style changed and we were required to keep two Hunters and pilots on standby during daylight hours; and our small, but surprisingly effective mobile air defence radar also on continuous watch during daylight hours.

One day Vaughan and I were on standby when a target appeared over the Yemen, heading straight for the border. Colonel Saud would not let me take off until he had instructed the guns in Najran to stand down, in case they shot at us. He couldn't get through on the telephone and the Egyptian IL-28 bombed Najran in broad daylight from about 10,000'. I could hardly contain myself; all the training of fighter pilots worldwide is never used by 99.9% of them because there are quite simply no aeroplanes to shoot down. Yet here we were with a target, two experienced pilots, and two of the loveliest of all interceptors and we were not allowed to fly. The next day Vaughan and I were again on standby when Les Murray our elderly small, wizened, delightful and top class fighter controller came through on our intercom, "I cannot believe this Tony, I have an identical return tracking to the border. You must get down to Najran in case they are stupid enough to do it again." I rushed into Colonel Saud's office scattering goat herdsmen, tea makers and drinkers. The Colonel still could not get through to the Army and without clearance into their air defence gun zone we could not fly. Finally, in desperation I told him we would fly and he could give us clearance when we were airborne; we had wasted five minutes already. Vaughan and I raced to our Hunters. Both of us did the same – we leaped aboard, started the engines, taxiied out and took off downwind with our straps undone for the first and only time in my life. Quite frankly, neither action is a good idea. By the time we were approaching Najran all eighteen connections required by a Hunter to nurture its pilot were done up, a short touch of the trigger had proved our four 30mm cannon and left the usual faint trace of cordite in the cockpit and then - dismay. In my mind's eye I can still see today a long line of bombs that were exploding, sending their mini mushrooms high into the still autumn sky; we must have been five miles or about 30 seconds flying time away and our IL-28 had just popped back over the border. I was terribly fond of Colonel Sammi who had only done what he was supposed to, but wars are not won by doing what you are supposed to. His five minutes of prevarication had cost Vaughan and me Colonel Rais' bag of gold which he had promised for any bomber shot down.

A fortnight later Colonel Sammi authorised me to take a pair of Hunters to Najran to show the locals that they were now well protected. I was leading Ron Allan and we crossed over the bombed village, for it was little more than a village, at about 15,000' and then turned to run down the valley. At that point the good Colonel told me that there were two MiG-15s after us and we were to stay clear of the area. A little late. We were down to 5,000', and descending at a good .9M. I hadn't counted on MiGs (which were rumoured to be flown by Ivans) but perhaps I would get a MiG kill after all. I slackened my shoulder harness to look behind me and as I did so I noticed lines of twinkling lights from the palm trees lining the Wadi. When I looked behind me for the MiGs, there was a line of black puffs of exploding Anti Aircraft Artillery shells, clearly radar guided as they followed, precisely, my descending track and were closing on me. At that point Ron told me what was happening. He had been flying in a wide tactical No.2 position and realised that the devilish MiGs were none other than ourselves. The Colonel was really sorry and said that firing on its friends was typical of their army: I agreed with him that ours was little better.

The Arab/Israeli war broke out in 1967 and, to my relief, we were grounded. Shooting down a vintage jet bomber flown by an Egyptian without fighter escort was one thing. Taking on a squadron of Mirage IIIs flown by angry Israelis did not appeal at all and was quite another matter. Many years later I was a guest at lunch in the RAF Museum; the other guest had just retired as head of the Israeli Air Force. I told him he was lucky that I was grounded during the Six-Day-War otherwise I would have been obliged to shoot him down. "You would have had to have got behind me first," he replied with a smile. At that moment I thought that it would not have been a good idea to duel with him, whatever I was flying. And then our war slowed down; I suspect the diplomats had been talking. We had a four-ship display team which I led in the two-seater and then I flew a solo aeros slot. Vaughan was flying the Lightning now and he and I flew a mirror formation. I was flying the Hunter inverted and Vaughan slid forward under me, but not too close, in case the low pressure over the Lightning sucked me down on to him. The Colonel thought it was terrific.

There was a small insurrection on the Hunter flight. I organised the flying programme and someone had noticed that every month I was flying more hours than anyone else. I promised not to and by the last day of the next month all the others' hours were equal and I was only a whisker behind them. I was on the 0600 standby and at 0900 there was a scramble to Najran; it was a false alarm but we landed back with 2 hours 40 mins logged. We were due for relief at 1300 and then at 1240 there was another scramble back to Najran, again to set up the same cab rank patrol pattern, but this time I was on my own as the other Hunter failed to start. Nothing happened so perhaps the Russians and their Egyptian friends wanted to see if we had got our act together and were checking our response time. By the time I had landed I was an unassailable 'hog of the month' with five hours more than anyone else and completely in the clear of authorising extra flying for myself.

One of the Lightning pilots was Vic Wightman, a QFI (Qualified Flight Instructor) on type and Vaughan had seen my tongue hanging out with longing as the Lightning had so far eluded my log-book. There was plenty of time at Khamis so for a week and a bit I learnt the systems, the numbers, the emergencies and, last but not least, asked a myriad of questions; finally I was ready for my ground school examination. By the time a jet aircraft gets to squadron service all the 'nasties' have been identified and either engineered out or become no-go areas, so any squadron pilot should have no trouble in flying any new type. It will be strange and the first few sorties will be quite tense as the brain struggles to fly the aircraft normally and suppress the anxiety that it has forgotten something. I was very well prepared by the time Vic and I got going but had not flown a simulator which makes first solos much more relaxed affairs. The aircraft was a dream to fly albeit with its legendary acceleration and climb performance much reduced by operating at a density altitude of up to 13,000' because of the heat and height of the airfield. I didn't mind. Vaughan asked the Colonel to authorise my solo but alas he would not. I flew a total of six dual sorties - just enough to get a feel for the aircraft as a flying machine. I was impressed with a full reheat climb, horrified at the pathetic endurance, and surprised at how long it took to accelerate up to its limit of 1.7M. (The next time I flew as fast was at Mach 2 with 1440 mph indicated on the ground speed read out, a second lobster thermidor on its way from the galley and my Dom Perignon glass awaiting a refill). The RSAF had a flight of F-86 Sabres to the north of us and I tried to get the Colonel to arrange some dissimilar air combat with them but he wouldn't co-operate of course. I had hoped to fly the F-86 as part of a mutual familiarity programme but it didn't work. Oh, well, nothing venture nothing gain.

Shortly before the end of my contracted time a Saudi, Prince Abdullah, joined us. Some of the Saudi pilots we experienced were not very good aviators but 'Ab', as we knew him, was exceptional. One day Ab and I flew the two-seat Hunter. I navigated round the Yemen border while he flew the aircraft; he flew it much too low, I suspect to provoke a reaction or to prove something, but I sat impassively by saying only 'left up this Valley', 'right at that small hill', hoping only that he didn't hit the ground. He didn't, but I had probably been unwise in letting him erode any safety margin which, in aviation, if practiced regularly, is a sure passport to an early demise.

Ted Clowes, another new pilot, joined the Hunter flight, a delightful easygoing personality without a lot of natural ability. To test Prince 'Ab' I arranged a practice air combat session with Ted and myself in the T.7 and Ab in a single-seater. Ab's F.6 had much more power but the absence of heavy armament in the two-seater meant that it was a difficult proposition for an F.6 if it was well flown. It was an unusual day for Arabia as there was some cloud about, but the exercise got under way as normal. In a short time it was quite obvious to me that our Saudi Royal was going to have us fair and square; I had briefed Ted on the principle of the so called 'high G Barrel roll' as a defensive/aggressive manoeuvre, and when the time was right I told him to initiate it. He screwed up and we fell into the only cloud for miles around. When we fell out of it there was our poor Abdullah, right in front of us. I unkindly called for a formation rejoin and when he said that he had lost sight of us an unpleasant streak in me enjoyed saying, "We are right behind you." Abdullah wasn't with us for long; he announced that he was going to Jeddah to collect a private aircraft. Someone said "I thought people weren't allowed private planes in Saudi." "People aren't," he rejoined. I liked his style.

For most of the time Khamis had been a building site and the pilots' accommodation was nearly the last to be completed. We each had our own room with screened windows to keep out the nastier bugs, but I was more concerned at the prospects of the huge camel spiders which I knew would emerge after any rain looking for locust hoppers. In February 1968 it rained. I went to bed with a wet towel along the bottom of the door, turned onto my front where I always sleep, tried not to think of all the sex I was missing by not being in London, and was nearly asleep when I felt a huge spider running up my right leg. As I brought my hand down to hit it, it bit me. Of all the luck, I, the only arachnophobic pilot at Khamis, the only one who had taken enormous care to block the crack under my door had not only had a spider in his room but actually on him. I removed the corpse and looked for the unauthorised entry point. Under my bed the floor had been broken by the contractors, and not repaired, allowing the intruder into my room. I was very proud of the two little puncture marks on my leg which of course were quite harmless. Camel spiders eat locusts and scorpions, they are 'wolf' spiders and non-toxic but at least I had a war wound. Sadly I doubt if, even in the USAF, it would have qualified me for a Purple Heart.

I had some leave due and, to cut a long story short, my long term girlfriend who, over the seven years that I had known her must have dumped me five times, had returned from Singapore where she had spent a year working for the Foreign Office. I asked her to marry me and she said she would. Most strange. I then returned to Saudi until March 31st 1968 when our contract ended.

UK tax law at the time produced some weird effects: I had to be out of England until April 6th to avoid tax on my income and my similar-sized gain on the Vehicle and General Insurance company shares. I took a five-day break in Milan with another ex-Hill Samuel and old school-friend David Lockwood; officially I was helping him to prepare his year-end accounts but all I can dimly remember of the visit was conducting a survey at 2am one morning into Milanese prostitution. I landed at Heathrow at 8am on April 6th and eventually was required by the Inland Revenue to produce documentary proof of my flight including the date, the airline and the time of touchdown. Bastards! But I had them.

On April 25th 1968 I married Julia Wilkinson at the Brompton Oratory, South Kensington. The honeymoon was in Barbados and we lived happily ever afterwards, but that is another story.

The End

Appendix I

MY RAF FLYING SUMMARY FOR 7½ YEARS

A summary of my flying in seven and a half years in the RAF. Flight times are all 'wheels on wheels off' which is standard RAF but not civil practice where taxiing time is included. Section 'A' I flew as First Pilot and Captain, Section 'B' only in an aircrew capacity eg Second Pilot.

'A' JET FIRST PILOT

de Havilland	VAMPIRE	FB.5, FB.9, T.11	193.40
Hunting	JET PROVOST	T.1, T.2	97.15
Hawker	SEA HAWK	FGA.6 (Royal Navy)	3.15
Hawker	HUNTER	F.4, F.6, T.7, FGA.9	341.55
de Havilland	VENOM	FB.4	103.40
Gloster	JAVELIN	T.3, FAW.5, FAW.9	10.10
English Electric	CANBERRA	T.4	5.40
Gloster	METEOR	T.7, F.8, NF.14	487.15 1244.50

T = Trainer
F = Fighter
B = Bomber
N = Night
GA = Ground Attack

PISTON FIRST PILOT

Percival	PROVOST	T.1	30.00
de Havilland	CHIPMUNK	T.10	95.20 125.20

'B' PISTON MULTI ENGINED SECOND PILOT/DUAL

de Havilland	DEVON (Twin Eng Transport)	18.55
Avro	ANSON (Twin Eng Transport)	3.10
Scottish Aviation	TWIN PIONEER (Twin Eng Transport)	1.15
Douglas	DAKOTA (Twin Eng Transport)	.25
Vickers	VALETTA (Twin Eng Transport)	.40
Vickers	VARSITY (Twin Eng Transport)	.35
Auster Aircraft	AUSTER (Army Air Corps) Single Engine	3.05
Handley Page	HASTINGS (Four Eng Transport)	92.30 121.35
Total Hours		1491.45

Appendix II

MY POSTINGS AND UNITS 1956-1963

In all three services there is always a rapid movement of personnel through a variety of units during training. The frequency of my postings was normal until my first Squadron, No.63, was disbanded as part of the contraction of the RAF. This subsequently triggered a turbulent career.

1.4.56 – 4.4.56	CARDINGTON	BEDFORD	INDUCTION PROCESSS
5.4.56 – 3.7.56	KIRTON-IN-LINDSEY	LINCS	INITIAL TRAINING
3.7.56 – 3.4.57	HULLAVINGTON	WILTS	No.2 FTS.
12.4.57 – 4.12.57	SWINDERBY	LINCOLN	No.8 AFS
28.12.57 – 30.1.58	VALLEY	ANGLESEY	No.7 AFS
6.2.58 - 1.6.58	CHIVENOR	DEVON	No.229(F) OCU
10.6.58- 1.11.58	WATERBEACH	CAMBRIDGE	No.63(F) SQN
2.11.58- 4.5.59	DISHFORTH	YORKS	No.242 TCU (Hastings)
5.5.59 - 10.4.61	ADEN	YEMEN ARABIA	No.8 (DF/GA) SQN
NOV 59 – MAY 60	SALALAH	OMAN ARABIA	STATION ADJ
5.5.61- 21.7.61	BIRCHAM NEWTON	NORFOLK	JC and SS COURSE
22.7.61 – 27.7.61	LEEMING	YORKS	No.228 JAVELIN OCU
27.7.61- 22.9.61	OUSTON	NORTHUMBERLAND	ADC to AOC 11 Gp
22.9.61- 10.2.63	LECONFIELD	YORKS	ADC to AOC 11 Gp

AUGUST 1962	WEST RAYNHAM (CFE)	NORFOLK	CANBERRA CONV.
10.2.63- 29.2.63	MANBY	LINCS	PROVOST CONV.
1.3.63- 31.12.63	CHIVENOR	DEVON	No.229 OCU

Appendix III

UNITED KINGDOM RAF STATIONS

Saxa Vord Radar
(Shetland Island)

Aird Uig Radar

Lossiemouth

Buchan Radar

Leuchars

Boulmer Radar

Ouston

Middleton St George

Leeming

Dishforth

Leconfield

Patrington Radar

Valley

Swinderby

West Raynham (CFE)

Aberporth

Waterbeach

Hullavington

Hartland Radar

Chivenor

Ventnor Radar

Appendix IV

YEMEN

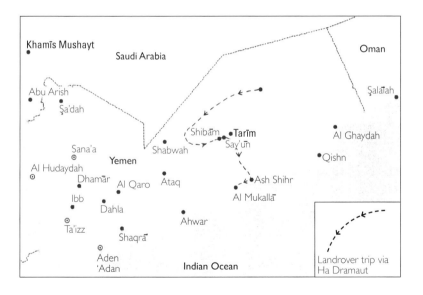

Khamīs Mushayt

Saudi Arabia

Oman

Abu Arish

Şa'dah

Şalālah

Shibām Tarīm

Al Ghaydah

Sana'a Yemen

Shabwah Say'ūn

Al Hudaydah

Qishn

Dhamār Al Qaro Ataq

Ash Shihr

Ibb

Al Mukallā

Ta'izz Dahla

Ahwar

Shaqrā

Aden 'Adan

Indian Ocean

Landrover trip via
Ha Dramaut

THE SEA TURBULENT
by Tony Haig-Thomas

AIR TEST No.10
(From VINTAGE AIRCRAFT MAGAZINE)

Norman Jones sat in the crew room of the Tiger Club carving yet another wooden spoon; a pile of chippings all over the floor testified to the fact that, in this sphere at least, British productivity was equal to anything the rest of the world had to offer. I sat at the other end drinking a cup of coffee and hoping that Neil Williams wouldn't find me and make me do yet another training session in the old Zlin 226, G-ATMZ, which was our aerobatic mount in those far-off days of twelve years ago.

"Ever flown a seaplane?" said Norman reverting to a vigorous bout of sandpapering that had already covered everything with a fine film of fall out. "No Norman" I replied rather nervously, wondering what was coming next.

"Excellent, you are just the chap I need for some seaplane trials; I have had some floats made for the Turbulent and I don't want anyone flying it with any preconceived ideas about how to do it." Naturally I agreed, if I hadn't I might have been banned from the Cosmic Wind "Ballerina" that was, at that time, my relaxation from the aerobatic world. This was the first time that I had heard that floats were to be fitted to the Turbulent which I had of course already flown on wheels and skis and was to lead to one of the more pleasurable experiences of my flying days.

The concept was, of course, Norman's who had recruited Dr John Urmston to construct the floats from the designs of Ray Hillborne. John had recently completed building his Currie Wot, G-ARZW, and so was well qualified as a handyman, while Ray Hillborne acquired a book on float design, published in 1924, an appropriate period piece slide rule and, presumably, some drawing paper. Eighteen months passed before the hardware arrived at Horsey Island in the Walton-on-the-Naze backwaters while back at Croydon Rollasons had modified Turbulent G-

ARJZ. They had fitted a 50 hp engine, moved the pitot/static sensor onto the port wing, added a few metal rigging points onto the fuselage and, finally, a small handle in the cockpit on the starboard wall. This, if pulled vigorously, removed the skin from the pilot's knuckles and rotated the engine very slowly; certainly far too slowly to ever start a reluctant Ardem VW conversion.

A fortnight after my recruitment as a development test pilot I stood anxiously on the west end of Horsey Island awaiting the arrival of the Turbulent (on wheels) with Norman at the helm. I had cleared the runway of the bales of hay, the wind sock sported a moderate angle of droop right down the west-east runway and then, spot on ETA, the little yellow aircraft buzzed into sight, turned upwind and, to my surprise, landed downwind well up the runway. It trundled down to the end of the strip before hitting a pile of hay bales right on the edge of a very deep lake. Norman climbed out and removed his deerstalker, thermos and sandwiches (carried in case of forced landings). "Morning Tony, lovely day" said Norman, completely ignoring the immersion in water that he had missed by six feet due to the timely presence of the bale barrier. "Just take her up and make sure she's alright."

"Right Norman" I replied. Being fresh out of the Air Force I obeyed orders without question and anyway the aeroplane looked intact. We turned it round, swung the prop and off I went, the aircraft being parked at the downwind end of the runway. This was rather tactless and perhaps it would have been more polite to have taxied to the upwind end and taken off downwind, pretending that Norman had landed correctly. Airmanship however overcame a desire to please the Club chairman and a 15 knot downwind component would probably have meant exceeding VNE on the ground before I got airborne, which seemed a dubious proposition.

After landing, John Urmston, Norman and I pulled the "Turb" over the sea wall and fitted the floats in half an hour; it looked terrific. Norman insisted on doing the first flight and when the tide was high after lunch, which included plenty of liquid to quell any lingering doubts we might have had, we set off. Norman taxied out, took off, turned downwind and landed, then John did the same and, finally, it was my turn.

I strapped in, started up and taxied out using a lot of power and rudder as there were no water rudders fitted. There was a very strong weathercock tendency which could only be resolved by high speed and power. The aircraft felt really great and had, in my mind's eye, already become an S.6b as my initial apprehension gave way to the more usual over confidence, helped no doubt by the lunchtime grape. I arrived in the open water, turned into wind, opened the throttle and surged forward up onto the step and then, at around 55 kts, the immutable laws of nature took over – thrust equalled drag – I covered another three hundred yards, which seemed reasonable as the runway stopped at Holland – 75 miles away – and then, remembering that seaplanes were always difficult to unstick, I jerked the stick back and the aircraft popped off the water like a cork from the Moet & Chandon and hour or so earlier. Speed was still 55 kts; I climbed ahead levelled off and accelerated – still only 55 kts. I began to wonder whereabouts on the drag curve I was exactly. Try a turn, no problems here, speed decayed slightly just a knot or two, slight loss of directional stability while other axes appeared unchanged. I reduced power a little, speed still 55 kts; no wonder Norman had said that 55 kts was a good approach speed, the aircraft seemed to fly at nothing else. I did a couple of figure eights and then lined up for the landing, reduced power a little and holding the by now magic figure flew the little aircraft down to about 20 – 30 feet and then allowed it to sink down until the rear of the floats cut the surface of the water with a glorious hissing sound. As the speed decayed I cut the power and the aircraft came down off the step and settled gratifyingly forward in the water. I was a seaplane pilot.

In conclusion, I would say that an aeroplane on floats is not much fun when airborne but the water handling and take-off and landing are terrific and should be experienced by all lovers of proper aeroplanes. No wonder so many aircraft had floats in the '20s and '30s when they really understood proper flying.

Author's Note

In case any of this should be read at Aviation House, Gatwick, I would like to add that all events are, of course, entirely fictitious and in any case the statute of limitations means that after twelve years we have got away with it.

POSTSCRIPT

Sometimes I read a flying biography and, apart from being left feeling pathetic after the tales of derring-do, I get irritated when, at the end, it says 'the author never flew again and became a successful businessman'. Successful how, and in what trade or profession? Was he a manufacturer of machine tools in Augsburg or did be make blue films in Hamburg? I feel that I should be told. I like German biographies best as their pilots were not taken off ops and rested like our aircrew, they just flew and either survived or were killed. Few survived but those that did have wonderful stories to tell, but seldom say what they did when they stopped flying. This is the justification for my postscript, not advanced egomania.

Briefly then my flying career, and involvement with aeroplanes, became much less interesting, but much more varied, after my marriage in 1968 at the age of thirty. I had noticed that Tiger Moths were being bought by Americans in increasing numbers together with some of the rarer lepidoptera. With this in mind it seemed to be a good idea to form a small group to buy and preserve one of each type of Moth that remained and I asked Robin D'Erlanger and James Baring (now Revelstoke) if they would like to form a syndicate to do so. Their sympathies for my mental health were much appreciated but what I really wanted was money; I had to make do with sympathy. Undeterred I pressed on alone and bought Moth Minor G-AFNG for £400 on condition that I took on liability for another one (G-AFNI) that was dismantled and stored at Rochester for which I was to be charged £1 a month. To save this financial haemorrhage I gave G-AFNI away – not very clever, with hindsight. Next I bought a Tiger Moth for £500 and then a Hornet Moth (G-ADLY) for £800. At this stage I had been married for three years, had four children, two girls and twin boys, and had started my own business in the City money markets. Julia and I had also bought a derelict Queen Anne manor house in the village just South of Horsey Island where I had spent my youth. An action packed

1000 days. The aeroplane collecting continued with a Fox Moth (G-ACEJ) and a Gipsy Moth (G-ATBL) for £3000 each. These were followed by a Puss Moth (G-AEOA) also for £3000 and then at last, in 1976, Leopard Moth (G-ACLL) for £7500. The 1970's inflation had really set in by this time.

I had all seven de Havilland Moths restored by Cliff Lovell in Hampshire and then, in 1978, I took them to the Shuttleworth Collection and flew a seven ship formation on a very windy day at one of their displays. John Cadd had been the photographer on a diving expedition to Alta Fiord in northern Norway, where I had been one of the divers. He had made a film of our expedition's efforts to find and raise the midget submarine X7, one of the four man X-craft that had been lost while attacking the Tirpitz. John had made an excellent film so I retained him to film the Moth Balbo. When it was all done I decided to sell the collection and buy a small three bed roomed house in Chelsea with the proceeds. I had read in the Economist that house prices in Chelsea had fallen for seven years, and were now very cheap. We still have the house and, when I see it, I think of that windy day at Old Warden and the ten years of my life that it took to collect Sir Geoffrey de Havilland's Moths.

Having got rid of my Moths, I bought a Harvard, which I kept for nineteen years, and in which both my sons logged over a hundred hours. A Piper Cub followed because all my friends seemed to have one and we still have it thirty years later, and finally, last but not least, a de Havilland Dragonfly, twin engined, 1935, executive aircraft. I had persuaded Martin Barraclough to a joint-venture with the Dragonfly as there were none left flying in the world and I did not feel inclined to do it by myself. Eventually the Harvard and Dragonfly were sold and I bought a Grumman Avenger. The Avenger, 'Fat Charlie' as I called it, had a 1900 hp, 44 litre, 14 cylinder Wright Cyclone and was a very noisy US Navy torpedo bomber; I owned it for nineteen years also and eventually sold it to a man in Switzerland where it now, at the time of writing, lives at Lausanne.

In 1976 I had become a Shuttleworth pilot which allowed me to fly numerous types of aircraft from pre-First World War, First World War, 1930 military classics (like the Hawker Hind, Gloster Gladiator and Westland Lysander) through to the de Havilland Chipmunk and Percival Provost trainers of the fifties. In 1971 I had told my, even then, long suffering aeronautical widow that my sole ambition was to run the

Shuttleworth Collection. In 1995, at a dinner in London, Micky Astor asked me if I would succeed as Aviation Trustee with a brief to stop the Collection losing money. It was an unpaid job that has given me great pleasure ever since. I remained on the Collection pilot list for a total of 28 years.

The end of the Cold War had seen numerous ex-military jets come on the market. These were mainly Jet Provost variants and in the early nineties I became an instructor (unpaid) to the private owners at North Weald. This gave me another 1000 hours of jet time on Jet Provost, Vampire, Hunter, Venom, L.29, and T-33 aircraft. Most agreeable. On the fiftieth anniversary of my first solo in a Jet Provost I gave a party for all my old Course from Hullavington. Jim Baldwin (Canberras and Vulcans) and I each did a take off, a loop, a roll, and a landing in a Jet Provost. Jim and I share our birthdays (19.11.37) and had each flown our first solos on that same day in July 1956. Although I am now seventy and a retired businessman I commute to North Weald in my Piper Cub and fly, when I am asked to, the aircraft types of my youth.

My business was eventually sold to a Swiss Group. I ran the international broking division and another old RAF and Eton friend, Eric Schurman, ran the bank. The love of my life from my teens and early twenties had gone on her way to be replaced by a new and much better one to whom I have now been married for forty years. We live in the same old Queen Anne manor house that is a little less derelict than it used to be and have seven grandchildren and counting. My log books now record 6500 hours on nearly 120 types and that, as they say, is that.

Tony Haig-Thomas
Kirby Hall
Kirby-le-Soken, Essex
November 2007

Old Fighter Pilots Never Die – They Just Get Fatter!
The author as Aviation Trustee of the Shuttleworth Collection with his management team.

A novel fund raising scheme has been tried. SVAS members were asked to 'Spot the Pompous Twit' and shown the photograph above . 368 members took part with the prize being a flight in the Lysander. Unfortunately no one won it. The correct answer should, of course, have been Captain Mainwaring.

Prop Swing Winter 2002